THE PROTEINS-FOR-PENNIES COOKBOOK

The
Proteins-for-Pennies
Cookbook

by John Woods

PETER H. WYDEN  PUBLISHER · NEW YORK

The Proteins-for-Pennies Cookbook
Copyright © 1974 by John Woods
All rights reserved, including the right to reproduce
this book, or parts thereof, in any form, except for
the inclusion of brief quotations in a review.

LIBRARY OF CONGRESS CATALOG CARD NUMBER: 74–79611
MANUFACTURED IN THE UNITED STATES OF AMERICA
ISBN: 0-88326-074-3

To everyone I love—and they know who they are

Contents

THE PROTEINS-FOR-PENNIES COOKBOOK

All About the Magic Little Bean

What natural food has almost three times the amount of protein as roast beef (but with none of its saturated fat content), one-third the calories, is rich in iron and the important minerals—and all for an unbelievably low price in comparison with what every housewife is having to pay for beef, eggs, and milk in these days of inflation and *more* inflation? Fortunately for us, the answer is something most of us have overlooked, perhaps never even considered. It's a magic little bean called the soybean.

But then it must taste like all those things that are supposed to be good for us. Wrong! Properly prepared, it will make all sorts of delicious dishes that are both tempting and wonderfully versatile. So the soybean is a sort of miracle vegetable, a natural source of protein, that could well spell the way to survival in the future. But first let me tell you all about it.

We Westerners have virtually ignored the soybean as food for humans, even though nutritionists have long ex-

1

tolled its incomparable virtues. Soybeans have twice the protein content of meat or fish, one and one-half times the protein content of cheese, three times the protein content of eggs, and eleven times the protein content of milk. They are low in carbohydrates and have little or no starch. Yet they contain the amino acids essential for maintaining human life. They are high in calcium, iron, phosphorus, potassium, and B vitamins (including B_1—thiamine—so necessary for daily energy!), and to make them even more irresistible to health-conscious (and heart-conscious) Americans, they contain lecithin, a fat emulsifier, that is helpful in controlling cholesterol build-up in the blood and vital organs. In fact, most of the commercial lecithin on the market comes from soybeans.

Another of the soybean's many qualities is its rich combination of *both* calcium and magnesium. And why is this important to the human body? Insufficient magnesium in the diet can cause large amounts of valuable calcium to be lost. Mother Nature, in so generously providing the soybean with its own supply of magnesium, has thus insured the utilization of all its valuable calcium. In short, this little bean is a miracle of nature. It is the only vegetable that is a true meat substitute.

It is one of the few foods containing complete proteins and *no saturated fats*! It is so potent and concentrated that a person could survive quite well for an extended period of time on a diet of nothing but soybeans. This fact alone may give pause to anyone concerned with the current crises confronting us on this planet. Today, with the ecology problems, population explosion (200,000 new mouths to feed each day!), as well as the ever-threatening protein shortage, not to mention the spiraling costs of most staple foods, the soybean takes on vital, new importance. It's quite possible that most of us will become increasingly dependent on the soybean for the natural protein so crucial to health—indeed, to life! And why not, at only 130 calories per 100 grams?

To those of you with a more sophisticated palate, such a prospect may understandably seem dreary. It is unfortunate that soybeans have gained the reputation of being a "palatable" but somewhat bland health food product—nutritious to be sure, but not especially appealing to the taste buds. Or maybe just for those who don't know better. And if you have ever suffered through the usual soybean concoction created by a well-meaning friend (with "faddistic" tendencies), or if your own experiments have met with something less than enthusiasm at the family table, you may be nodding in agreement. However, I can assure you (and the recipes in this book prove it) that soybeans, properly prepared and seasoned, are every bit as delicious as they are nourishing. And that's quite a claim. Maybe it's because I was raised in Texas where food is traditionally very spicy, and from an early age I learned to tell the difference between dull—bland—food and what tastes delicious. Anyway, I grew up in Denton and I was fortunate enough to have a mother who is a superb cook. Among my favorite childhood memories (maybe not *yours*, but remember how different Texas can be) was coming home to find a tasty pot of beans, soybeans that is. For we grew up with soybeans, and that area continues to be one of the main sources of soybeans for this country. So, for your benefit and ready use, many of the recipes you will find in this book have been adapted from my family's menus.

The soybean has been called the Cinderella of today's food industry. Perhaps it is. Its meteoric rise from rags to riches has amazed growers, buyers, and importers—as well as Wall Street. The amazement is understandable considering that only ten years ago the plant was being grown by some farmers merely as a cover crop to enrich the soil: it was plowed under after reaching maturity. Today, the demand for soybeans on the world market has become so intense that it is impossible to keep pace with, and prices have soared accordingly.

Yet, this relative newcomer to the West has been a staple food product in the Orient for more than four thousand years. Detailed records of the planting and cultivation of soybean crops, written more than two thousand years before Christ, have been found in China. The soybean was considered sacred: in fact, it was known as one of the "Five Sacred Grains"—the others being wheat, rice, barley, and millet. Battles were fought for the choicest growing fields of Manchuria, where even today soybeans are cultivated. Indeed, the soybean is so closely associated with China that some historians attribute the survival of China as a nation to its use of the soybean as a food.

Today the Chinese and Japanese still consume vast amounts of soybean products, and soybean curd is one of the main sources of protein and calcium in their diet.

A Japanese friend of mine recently visited her native land after having spent eight years in the United States. She was amazed at the energy and stamina of the country people she saw. These people—farmers, field hands, carpenters, etc.—who work long, hard hours every day, depend heavily on soybeans, soybean curd, soy sprouts, and soybean paste for their sustenance. Their obvious good health and vitality were impressive.

It is believed that eighteenth-century missionaries returning from China brought the first soybeans to Europe. Early experiments to grow it were made in France and, later on, in Italy, but these were on a small scale. The soybean was first introduced to the United States in 1804. There are written reports of soybean crops flourishing in Pennsylvania as early as 1840. Around 1854 the Perry expedition to Japan brought back other strains of the soybean. Later the U.S. Department of Agriculture introduced hundreds of species of soybeans from Asia and Europe. Since 1952, when American farmers planted a mere 14 million acres of soybeans, the growth has been steady and phenomenal. In 1973, 54 million acres of soybeans were planted in the United States. This accounts for approximately 85 percent of the world's supply. Of course, the major part of this enormous harvest is refined into the highly prized soy meal —a super-protein food for cattle and poultry. However, when one considers the world's population explosion, pollution of the lakes and oceans, and the ever-growing demands for protein, a further dramatic statistic takes on even more significance. Simply stated, one acre of grazing land will yield 43 pounds of food protein as beef cattle eat its grass. This same acre planted in soybeans would yield 600 pounds of food protein. That is real food for thought!

The soybean is in itself a remarkably versatile food: it can be cooked for use in casseroles, salads, soups, stews, and omelets. It can be puréed and used in loaves, pies, cakes, and breads. It can be soaked in water and deep-fried to make a delightful, nutty snack. Or it can be totally transformed into milk, curds, or yogurt. And in the rest of this book you'll find out exactly how all this is done. But wait— there's even more! This miraculous bean can also be "sprouted," thus creating an always available fresh vegetable. It can be milled into flour—not *just* flour, but a flour so high in protein and other nutrients that it is considered by nutrition experts to be one of the most valuable of all foods. And finally, it can be crushed into "granules," creating yet another high-protein product that can be used in ever so many ways. Let's take a closer look at these wonderful products.

Soy flour comes from milled soybeans with or without the seed coat. It is creamy yellow, light and fluffy, and rather nutty in flavor. It is lighter than wheat flour—one cupful weighs about 75 grams as compared with 100 grams for soft-wheat flour or 113 grams for hard-wheat flour. If milled with the seed coat, there will be brown specks in the flour. Like whole-grain wheat, these specks are the ground-up hilum of the seed and in no way affect the quality of the flour. Since soy flour has no gluten and little or no starch, it cannot be used as a thickening agent in soup, sauces, etc. Nor can it be used alone in breads or cakes.

There are two types of soy flour on the market—full-fat and low-fat—and they are for the most part interchangeable in recipes. The full-fat flour is valuable for its rich content of healthful unsaturated vegetable oils and lecithin. It contains all the oil originally present in the raw soybeans —usually 18 to 20 percent *and* it's virtually starch-free. Full-fat flour also contains 40 to 45 percent protein and a rich supply of "antistress factors"—vitaminlike substances that markedly increase resistance to most (though not all) types of stress.

The low-fat flour has an astounding protein content of 47 to 54 percent. One cup of low-fat soy flour contains no less than 60 grams of complete protein! It is also lower in calories because of the reduction in oil.

These flours have numerous health-giving properties in common. Soy flour is one of the richest sources per pound of the entire B-vitamin complex. Compared to patent wheat flour, soy flour is fifteen times richer in calcium, seven times richer in phosphorus, ten times richer in iron, ten times richer in thiamine, nine times richer in riboflavin, five times richer in niacin, and four or five times richer in total minerals. And what's the price for this natural cornucopia of vitamins and minerals? At the time of writing, roughly 70¢ per pound (packaged) or 53¢ per pound from the bin. This easily makes it one of the least expensive sources of superprotein available. With this in mind, the following equivalents are even more convincing: one pound of soy flour contains as much protein as three pounds of boneless meat, or three dozen eggs, or seven and one-half quarts of milk, or two pounds of cheese.

Soy granules (or grits, as they are sometimes called) are made by grinding or otherwise crushing the soybean into small pieces. Often they are toasted, which gives them a delicate nutlike flavor. They are high in protein (50 percent) and, at the same time, very inexpensive. Compare the recent (1974) price for ground round beef—$1.80 per pound—with the recent price of soy granules—57¢ per pound. Impressive? But wait. The pound of soy granules has almost *three times more* protein than that pound of ground meat (beef is only about 18 percent protein). Very roughly, this means that a third of a pound of granules, which costs 19¢, is almost equal in protein content to the pound of ground beef, which costs $1.80. Impressive indeed, and hard to beat!

As you will see in Chapter 2, soy granules provide the quickest, easiest, and cheapest way for you to add protein to the diet.

Bean sprouts are used extensively in Japanese and Chinese cuisine and have been for centuries. Although they can be found in some markets, growing them is so simple and economical (one cup of dried beans will explode into two pounds of sprouts!) that everyone should learn to make them. Children are usually only too happy to take over this "experiment": the little miracle of nature that takes place is a fascinating process for them to observe as, over a period of days, the small dried beans swell, split open, and are gradually transformed into long delicate sprouts.

Bean sprouts are versatile: use them in salads, soups, stews, omelets, soufflés, casseroles, and fricassees. They are nutritious: they contain all the valuable nutrition of the soybeans plus an additional rich supply of vitamin C developed in sprouting. (The vitamin C content of soybeans increases more than 500 percent by the third day of sprouting!) Their fresh taste and crisp tenderness are delicious additions to any dish. Therefore, I have included a whole chapter on making dishes with bean sprouts.

In an emergency—when no other fresh vegetable is available—or in midwinter, a little "kitchen garden" of soybean sprouts would be most beneficial for the whole family. They are well worth the little effort required to produce them. Indeed, the only real "effort" is in remembering to water them.

Most of the recipes compiled here are utterly simple, classic bean recipes from all parts of the world—from Boston-baked to Rome's pasta e fagiòli. In fact, this book has such a variety of recipes from so many countries that one could almost call it a culinary tour of the bean world. I have also included some spicy examples from my native Texas, which are, however, distinctly Mexican in origin, as well as several inventions of my own. There are everyday family-style dishes, festive dishes, party dishes, exotic dishes, snacks, cakes, and pies—foods for every occasion. Each recipe is chock-full of high-quality soy protein in one form or another—the richest, most nutritious, and by far the most economical natural protein available. Just as important, if not more so, they all taste delicious!

You can give a great boost to your cooking as well as to your general health and well-being by serving soybeans often, either as a meat substitute or as a side dish. Try them —and enjoy them in good health.

General Note About Soy Products

All the soybean products used in the following recipes are generally available; increasingly, supermarket chains all over the country are stocking a wider variety of these products, and you will also find them in your local health food store. If you can't find exactly what you need, you might suggest to the supermarket manager that soybean products can easily be ordered. Or you could write yourself direct to the American Soybean Association, Box 158, Hudson, Iowa 50643, for the name of your nearest supplier.

Soybeans in the Kitchen

PREPARATION OF DRIED BEANS

Whether you buy the beans packaged in a supermarket or "from the bin" at a specialty store, remember to wash them thoroughly and pick them over to remove any foreign matter before you start on your recipe. They should be soaked overnight (or at least for several hours) regardless of which cooking method you choose; this will appreciably shorten the cooking time. To soak, put the beans in a large bowl or container and cover them with water, allowing 2 cups of liquid and 1 teaspoon of salt per cup of dried beans. After soaking, cook the beans in this water—do not pour it off as it has valuable food content.

The high protein content of soybeans requires them to be cooked longer than other beans. Of the three basic recipes, the quickest and easiest method is to use a pressure cooker—cooking time takes all of 45 minutes! Also, this is a considerable saving in fuel. The regular, top-of-the-stove method requires 4 to 5 hours cooking time. The third alternative—the freezer method—reduces the cooking time to about 2½ hours.

Pressure Cooker Method

Pour the soaked beans and the water used for preparing them into the pressure cooker. Cook for 45 minutes at 10 to 15 pounds pressure. The cooking time is the same for gaugeless pressure cookers.

Regular Method

Pour the soaked beans, with the water used for preparing them, into a cooking pot. Cover and simmer (do not boil) for 4½ to 5 hours, or until tender. Add more water as needed.

Freezer Method

Pour the soaked beans, with the water used for preparing them, into ice trays or freezing containers. The beans should be just covered with water. Freeze overnight, or as long as you like. Remove from freezer, place in a pot with sufficient water to cover. Cover and simmer (do not boil) for 2½ to 3 hours, or until tender. Add more water as needed.

Now proceed with the recipe you have chosen.

USEFUL COOKING HINTS FOR BEANS

One pound of dried soybeans is equal to 2¾ cups.
One pound of dried soybeans will make about 6 cups of cooked beans.

In other words, 1 cup of dried beans equals slightly more than 2 cups of cooked beans. This will be most helpful in preparing any recipe that requires precooked beans (as most of the following recipes do).

If you eat soybeans regularly, or if you have a large family, you will find it both a great time-saver and most convenient to cook 2 pounds of soybeans at a time. It's a great energy-saver too! This comes to slightly more than 12 cups of cooked soybeans. They keep perfectly well in the refrigerator for several days and of course can be frozen if you prefer. If you have a stock of precooked beans in the refrigerator, most of the following recipes can be prepared in a matter of minutes.

Properly cooked soybeans are as tender as any other bean; however, they will not become mushy or "cook-up," which is a distinct advantage in preparing salads, casseroles, or soups.

Soybeans will absorb quite a bit of water while cooking. Keep a kettle handy and add hot water as necessary.

If you like, add a bay leaf to any of the three basic recipes. It will give a delicate flavor to the beans and makes a pleasant cooking aroma.

Weights, Measures, and Equivalents

3 teaspoons	1 tablespoon
2 tablespoons	1 fluid ounce
16 tablespoons	1 cup
1 cup	½ pint
2 pints	1 quart
4 cups	1 quart
4 quarts	1 gallon
16 ounces	1 pound
1 pound flour	3 cups
1 pound butter	2 cups
1 stick butter	½ cup
¼ pound grated cheese	1 cup
1 pound cheese	4½ cups

1 pound brown sugar . . . .   2 to 2⅔ cups
1 pound confectioners' sugar . . 2½ to 3 cups
1 pound granulated sugar . . . .   2 cups
1 pound rice . . . .   2 cups (yields 3 to 4 cups
                                      cooked rice)
1 square chocolate . . . .   1 ounce or 3 tablespoons
                                      grated chocolate
1 egg . . . .   ¼ cup (approx.)
5 eggs . . . .   1 cup
9 eggs . . . .   1 pound
8 to 10 egg whites . . . .   1 cup
16 egg yolks . . . .   1 cup

Oven Temperature Chart

	Degrees Fahrenheit	Degrees Centigrade
Slow oven	250°–325°	120°–165°
Moderate oven	325°–375°	165°–190°
Quick or hot oven	400°–450°	205°–230°
Very hot oven	450°–550°	230°–290°

1

❧ ❀ ❧

Casseroles

An easy way to get your moneysworth is this bacon casserole—my aunt always served it to us when we were small. It was one lunch we never missed!

Bacon-Soybean Casserole

5 cups cooked soybeans, drained
½ pound sliced bacon
1 medium onion, chopped
1 cup grated American cheese
1 10-¾-ounce can tomato soup
1 cup milk
3 tablespoons catsup
Salt and freshly ground black pepper to taste

Fry bacon until crisp and drain. Reserve 2 tablespoons bacon drippings, and sauté onion until tender in it.

Combine beans, crumbled bacon, onion, cheese, tomato soup, milk, catsup, and salt and pepper. Pour ingredients into 2-quart casserole. Bake at 375° F. for 45 minutes. Serves 6.

For most of the baked-bean recipes I recommend a long soak period (8 to 10 hours) *plus* freezing overnight. This reduces the baking time to the usual 6 to 8 hours required for baked beans. To hasten the defrosting process, put frozen beans in a saucepan and heat slowly. When completely defrosted, drain beans in a colander. Remember to reserve the stock.

The next three recipes included here are classics and well worth what may seem at first glance some time and effort. Soybeans are especially suited to baking—they absorb the flavor through and through, yet do not cook to pieces in the process.

Boston-Baked Soybeans

½ pound slab bacon
1 onion, coarsely chopped
1 pound dried soybeans, soaked, frozen, and drained
3 tablespoons sugar
⅓ cup molasses (blackstrap)
½ teaspoon dry mustard
1 tablespoon salt

Preheat oven to 350° F.

Cut bacon into small cubes and brown in skillet. Drain and put into a 2-quart bean pot. Add onions and then pour in beans. Mix remaining ingredients in 2 cups of reserved stock and pour over beans. If necessary, add more stock or water until beans are just covered. Bake in oven for 6 to 8 hours. Add boiling water as necessary to keep beans just covered.

Serves 4 to 6.

Jamaican-Baked Soybeans

¾ pound salt pork, cut into ½-inch cubes
1 medium onion, studded with 6 cloves
1 pound dried soybeans, soaked, frozen, and drained
3 tablespoons sugar
⅓ cup molasses (blackstrap)
¼ cup dark rum
2 teaspoons dried mustard
1 tablespoon salt
1 teaspoon freshly ground black pepper
Pinch of thyme

Preheat oven to 350° F.
Brown salt pork in skillet, drain, and set aside.

Place onion in bottom of bean pot. Cover with half the drained beans and then a layer of half the salt pork. Add remainder of beans, and top with remaining salt pork.

Combine sugar, molasses, rum, mustard, salt and pepper, and thyme. Mix with ½ cup reserved stock and pour the mixture over beans. Add more stock to cover beans, if necessary. Cover and bake in preheated oven for about 6 hours, or until tender.

Add heated stock or water as necessary to keep beans just covered with liquid.

Serves 4 to 6.

Soybeans Bretonne

1 pound dried soybeans
2 cups stewed and strained tomatoes, mashed
2 cups chicken stock
1 14-ounce can of pimientos (diced bean-size)
2 onions, chopped
3 or 4 cloves garlic, minced
½ cup melted butter
  Salt to taste

Cook beans until tender using any one of the basic methods. Drain. Place in a bean pot and add all other ingredients. Cook covered for about 8 hours at 300° F.
Serves 6 to 8.

Soybeans and Cheese

Sauce:
  1 tablespoon butter
  1 tablespoon onion, finely chopped
  1 tablespoon flour
1¼ cup hot milk
  1 cup grated Swiss or Cheddar cheese
  ¼ teaspoon salt
  ⅛ teaspoon white pepper
    Pinch of nutmeg

  4 cups cooked soybeans, drained
  3 tablespoons bread crumbs

In small, heavy saucepan, sauté onion in butter. Stir in flour. Add milk, and cook over a medium flame, stirring constantly, until smooth. Add ½ cup of grated cheese, and stir constantly until melted. Then add salt, pepper, and nutmeg. Cook another 5 minutes.

Put soybeans in well-oiled casserole. Pour sauce over beans. Sprinkle the top with bread crumbs and the remaining ½ cup of cheese. Bake in 350° F. oven until sauce bubbles and the crumbs and cheese are golden brown.

Serves 4 or 5.

Buttered Soybeans and Carrots

2½ cups diced carrots
2 cups cooked soybeans, drained
½ cup water
½ teaspoon salt
2 tablespoons butter

Put all ingredients in a saucepan and simmer for 15 or 20 minutes. Serve hot.

Serves 4 or 5.

Soybeans Gratin

2 small onions, finely sliced
5 tablespoons butter
4 cups cooked soybeans, drained
1 slice ham, finely chopped (optional)
Salt and freshly ground black pepper
4 tablespoons bread crumbs

Preheat oven to 400° F.

Sauté onions in 2 tablespoons butter. Add the beans,

ham (optional), and salt and pepper. Sprinkle with bread crumbs. Melt remaining butter and drip over mixture. Bake in a preheated oven until bubbly and bread crumbs are browned.

Serves 4.

Now for some variety. The Japanese serve this dish on special occasions, for holidays, or one of their feast days. Its sweet and salty flavor will be a new taste sensation for most Westerners.

Kombu and Soybeans

2 cups dried soybeans
kombu (seaweed), equivalent to a 2-by-4-inch rectangle
1 carrot (diced bean-size)
1 package konnyaku (potato gelatine), diced bean-size (optional)
1 cup sugar
2 tablespoons soy sauce
2½ teaspoons salt

Prepare and cook the beans using any one of the three basic methods. Soak kombu for 30 minutes and cut into bean-size pieces. Add all the other ingredients, except for the seaweed, to the beans. Simmer until carrots are almost tender. Then add the seaweed and simmer for 20 minutes more.

Serves 4 or 5.

Note: Japanese seaweed and konnyaku are available in all oriental food stores and health food stores.

Soybeans Paprikash

4 tablespoons butter
2 cups thinly sliced onions
1 tablespoon paprika (or to taste)
¾ cup chicken broth
6 cups cooked soybeans, drained
Salt and freshly ground black pepper to taste
1 cup sour cream

Sauté onions in butter until translucent. Stir in paprika and mix well. Add chicken broth, beans, salt and pepper, and simmer for 20 to 25 minutes. Stir in sour cream but do not allow to boil. Then serve.

Serves 6 to 8.

Soybeans à la Madrilena

1 onion, chopped
3 tablespoons oil
1 teaspoon paprika
1 tablespoon parsley, chopped
½ cup dry white wine
1 tablespoon wine vinegar
3 cups cooked soybeans, drained
Salt and freshly ground black pepper to taste

Sauté onion in oil. Add paprika and parsley. Then add wine and vinegar. Stir well and let it bubble gently. Add beans, salt and pepper, and let simmer slowly for 20 minutes, stirring frequently. Add ¼ cup water if necessary to prevent sticking.

Serves 2 or 3.

Spanish-Style Soybeans

Sauce:
 1 small onion, minced
 ⅓ cup butter
 ½ cup flour
 ⅛ teaspoon nutmeg
   Salt and freshly ground black pepper to taste
 2½ cups chicken or beef broth
 3 egg yolks, slightly beaten
 2 tablespoons lemon juice

 ¼ cup parsley, finely chopped
 2 pimientos, chopped
 4 cups cooked soybeans, warmed

Sauté onion in 1 or 2 tablespoons butter. Blend in flour, nutmeg, and salt and pepper. Slowly stir in broth. Cook, stirring frequently, until mixture is thickened and smooth (about 10 or 15 minutes). Turn heat very low and blend in beaten egg yolks, the remaining butter, and lemon juice. Cook a few minutes more. Remove from heat, stir briskly, and add the parsley, pimientos, and the beans.
  Serves 6.

Note: This sauce may be made ahead—or in quantity—and stored (well-covered) in the refrigerator for several days. When ready to serve, simply heat sauce and beans together in oven.

Now for two traditional recipes from Mexico.
  If you ever yearn for Mexican food—and who doesn't —these two dishes are sure to satisfy. They are great for parties, but even better the second day!

Mexican Chili Beans

Sauce:

4 tablespoons olive oil
1 large onion, chopped
3 cloves garlic, chopped
2 hot Jalapeño peppers,* mashed
1 teaspoon salt
1 teaspoon oregano
1 tablespoon vinegar
1 tablespoon chili powder
1 cup hot water

1 pound soybeans, cooked using basic recipe with salt and
  bay leaf, and drained
1 cup grated Cheddar cheese

Heat oil and slowly cook onion and garlic. Add mashed
chili peppers, salt, oregano, vinegar, chili powder, and
water. Simmer together for 15 minutes.

Put beans in a greased casserole. Pour sauce over
beans, stir, and sprinkle with grated cheese. Bake in 350° F.
oven until cheese is melted.

Serves 8 to 10.

* Canned Jalapeño peppers can be bought in many markets.
If a milder sauce is desired, use only one Jalapeño pepper and 2
tablespoons chili powder.

Chili con Carne (with Soybeans)

  2 pounds dried soybeans
  1 bay leaf
⅔ cup olive oil
  4 medium onions, chopped
  4 or 5 cloves garlic, chopped
  3 pounds lean ground beef
  2 8-ounce cans tomato sauce
  5 tablespoons chili powder (or more)
  1 tablespoon oregano
1½ teaspoons cumin
    Salt and freshly ground pepper to taste

Simmer the washed and drained beans with a bay leaf for about 2 hours in a 10-quart saucepan. Heat oil in a large skillet; sauté onions and garlic until half-cooked, or limp but not transparent. Add chopped meat and brown lightly. Add the beef-onion mixture to partially cooked beans, along with tomato sauce and spices. Cover and continue cooking for about 3 hours more, or until beans are tender and mixture reaches a rich brown consistency. Add salt and freshly ground black pepper to taste. Remove cover during the last hour or so of cooking.

Serves 10 to 15.

Soybean and Rice Casserole (with Beef)

2 onions, chopped
2 tablespoons bacon drippings
1 pound lean ground beef
   Salt and freshly ground black pepper to taste
2 cups canned tomatoes, undrained and mashed
2 cups cooked soybeans, drained
2 cups firmly cooked rice, drained

Preheat oven to 350° F.

Sauté onions in bacon drippings. Add ground beef and fry until almost done, forking through frequently. Add salt and pepper and tomatoes. Simmer for about 5 minutes, stirring frequently.

Mix in soybeans and rice, pour into a greased casserole, and bake in oven for about 30 minutes.

Serves 6 to 8.

Here's an unusual recipe from East Africa—easy to make and fun to serve.

Soybeans in Peanut Sauce

  1 onion, chopped
  1 tablespoon oil
  1 tomato, chopped
  ½ cup peanuts, finely ground *OR* ½ cup peanut butter
  1 green chili pepper, minced
  2 cups cooked soybeans, drained
    Salt to taste
  1 cup water

In a heavy saucepan, lightly sauté onion in oil. Add tomato, peanuts or peanut butter, and chili pepper. Blend with fork and continue sautéing for about 5 more minutes. Add beans, salt to taste, and water. Cover and simmer for 20 to 30 minutes.

Serves 4.

Or you may want to try this Italian variety!

Escarole and Soybean Casserole

  1 head escarole (1½ pounds)
  2 tablespoons olive oil
  1 clove garlic, minced
  1 cup fresh or canned tomatoes
  2 cups cooked soybeans, drained
  1 teaspoon salt (or to taste)
    Freshly ground black pepper to taste

Remove tough or faded outer leaves of escarole. Separate well and wash thoroughly. Drain.

Boil escarole for 10 to 15 minutes, chopping up if necessary to put in saucepan, and drain, reserving ½ cup (or more) cooking liquid.

Heat oil and gently sauté garlic for 2 or 3 minutes. Add tomatoes, beans, salt and pepper, and ½ cup (or more) of cooking liquid. Simmer for 5 minutes.

Add cooked escarole and simmer for 8 to 10 minutes more.

Serves 4 to 6.

Kielbasa and Soybeans

1 pound kielbasa (Polish sausage) or catechino (Italian sausage)
6 scallions, including tops, finely chopped
¼ cup olive oil
1 cup parsley, finely chopped
6 cloves garlic, finely chopped
5 cups cooked soybeans, drained
½ cup dry white wine
Salt and freshly ground black pepper to taste

Place the sausage in a saucepan, add enough water to cover, and simmer for about 45 minutes.

Lightly sauté the chopped scallions in olive oil in a saucepan. Add ½ cup of parsley, the garlic, beans, wine, and salt and pepper. When the sausage is done, remove enough of the cooking liquid and add to beans to just barely cover.

Cook for about 10 minutes over low flame, stirring frequently.

Remove skin from sausage, cut into slices, and stir into the beans. Sprinkle with remaining parsley and serve.

Serves 6 to 8.

Brittany Soybeans

3 slices bacon, cut into small pieces
2 cups chopped tomatoes
2 cups diced potatoes
2 cups cooked soybeans, drained
　Salt and freshly ground black pepper to taste
1 can berberechos* (small clams), drained

　Fry bacon pieces until transparent, add tomatoes, and cook for 10 minutes. Then add the potatoes, beans, salt and pepper. Cover and let simmer until the potatoes are done. Add the drained berberechos to the potato-bean mixture, and cook for 10 minutes more. Mix well and serve.
　Serves 4 to 6.

This recipe comes from Ghana, on Africa's west coast. If the ingredients seem a little surprising at first, don't be timid. It's a refreshing and most satisfying taste.

* Progresso's small clams (*vongoli*) will do.

Soybeans and Dried Codfish

6 cups cooked soybeans, drained
½ pound dried cod (soaked overnight)
1 cup vegetable oil
1 large onion, minced
2 large tomatoes, chopped
2 tablespoons tomato paste
½ to 1 teaspoon ground red pepper (or to taste)
Salt
Boiled rice

Beans can be ground or left whole. Put the soaked cod in fresh cold water and bring to a boil. Reduce heat and cook until fork-tender. Heat the oil, and sauté chopped onion and tomatoes. Add tomato paste and pepper. Mix well. Drain fish and add to mixture. Then stir in beans (whole or ground). Add salt if necessary. Simmer in a covered skillet for about 30 minutes. Add boiling water if mixture gets too thick.

Serve this dish with boiled rice.

Serves 4 to 6.

Variation: One-half pound stew meat can be substituted for dried fish. Cut into small cubes, brown in oil, add a little water, and simmer until tender. Add to onion and tomato mixture, add beans, etc.

Lamb Curry with Soybeans

2½ cups chopped onions
3 garlic cloves, minced
2 tablespoons Indian curry powder (or to taste)
1½ teaspoons salt
1 cup yogurt
2 pounds lamb, cut in 1-inch cubes
¼ pound butter
1 pound cooked soybeans, drained
1½ cups boiling water

Mix together the onions, garlic, curry powder, salt, and yogurt. Add the lamb, tossing until lamb is completely coated with the curry mixture. Let stand for 1 hour.

Melt butter in a casserole or Dutch oven. Add meat and cook over low heat for about 25 minutes, stirring frequently. Stir in beans and boiling water. Cover and continue cooking over low heat for 30 minutes, or until meat is tender.

Serves 8 to 10.

Soybean Goulash

1 medium onion, chopped
1 tablespoon oil
1 pound ground beef
3 cups cooked soybeans, drained
1 8-ounce can tomato sauce
¼ cup catsup or chili sauce
Salt and freshly ground black pepper to taste

Sauté onion in oil. Add ground beef and brown until almost cooked through. Drain off excess fat if necessary. Add the remaining ingredients. Cover and simmer for 15 minutes.

Serves 4.

Soybeans, Indian Style

¼ cup butter
2 medium onions, chopped
1½ teaspoons turmeric
½ teaspoon powdered ginger
¼ teaspoon dried mint, or 6 leaves fresh mint
½ teaspoon dried hot red peppers
2 tomatoes, chopped
6 cups cooked soybeans, drained
1½ cups beef bouillon
  Bean stock
  Salt to taste

In a casserole, heat butter and sauté onions until transparent. Add turmeric, ginger, mint, hot red peppers, and tomatoes and mix well. Simmer for 10 minutes. Then add the soybeans, beef bouillon, and enough stock to cover beans. Salt to taste. Cover and simmer on top of stove for about 20 minutes.
Serves 6 to 8.

Soybeans and Ham in Red Wine

1 onion, finely chopped
1 green pepper, seeded and finely chopped
3 tablespoons butter
1 cup diced cooked ham
½ 8-ounce can tomato sauce
1 cup dry red wine
1 cup beef stock
5 cups cooked soybeans, drained
  Salt and freshly ground black pepper to taste

Sauté onion and green pepper in butter until onions are transparent. Add diced ham and cook a few minutes

more. Mix wine with tomato sauce, add to onion mixture, and season with salt and pepper. Simmer gently for 8 to 10 minutes. Add beef stock and beans. Cover and simmer for about 25 minutes more.
Serves 6.

A version I particularly enjoy is this one from Israel—and it's so practical.

Soybeans in Tomato Sauce

3 large onions, chopped
3 cloves garlic, minced
3 carrots, chopped
6 large ripe tomatoes
4 tablespoons or more olive oil
   Bean stock
¼ teaspoon cayenne
   Salt and freshly ground black pepper to taste
1 pound cooked soybeans, drained
½ cup parsley, minced

Sauté vegetables, including the garlic, in oil until tender. Add a little stock to moisten and cook to a pulp (10 to 15 minutes). Add seasonings. Now mix in beans and parsley with vegetable sauce and simmer together for about 15 minutes or more. Add more stock if necessary to prevent any sticking to the pan.
Serves 8 to 10.

Here is a very tasty and different way to use up leftover roast.

Soybeans, Portuguese Style

    2 cups leftover roast meat, cubed
1½ cups beef broth
   ½ cup port wine
    5 cups cooked soybeans, drained
      Salt and freshly ground black pepper to taste
    2 tablespoons butter
      Grated nutmeg to taste

Heat the meat and broth in a heavy saucepan. Add port wine and let simmer a few minutes. Add beans, cover, and simmer for 30 minutes more. Add salt and pepper, butter, and nutmeg.

Serves 6.

Don't fail to make this recipe. Follow the simple directions, but don't taste until finished! You will be most pleasantly surprised with the fresh flavor. This, incidentally, comes from Israel.

Soybeans with Apples

    3 cups cooked soybeans, drained
    4 medium cooking apples, peeled, cored, and quartered
    1 cup sugar
   ¼ pound butter
    1 teaspoon salt
   ½ cup red wine
    2 tablespoons wine vinegar
      Dash of cinnamon

Put all ingredients into a saucepan, mix well, cover, and stew gently over low flame for 1 hour. This can also be served cold, but it's best hot and steaming.

Serves 4 to 6.

Beans à la Jerezana

    4 cups cooked soybeans, drained
    2 medium onions, finely chopped
    4 tablespoons butter
    ½ pound diced ham
    ¾ cup sherry wine
    3 tomatoes, coarsely chopped
    2 tablespoons minced parsley
      Bouquet of spices*
      Salt and freshly ground black pepper to taste

Sauté onions in butter until golden brown. Add ham and heat. Then add sherry, tomatoes, parsley, spice bouquet, and salt and pepper. Let simmer for about 10 minutes. Add beans and heat together thoroughly.

Serves 4 to 6.

To make bouquet of spices:
Take a 3-inch square of doubled cheesecloth and in the center put: ¼ teaspoon oregano, ¼ teaspoon sage, ¼ teaspoon rosemary, ¼ teaspoon basil, 1 bay leaf (crumbled). Make a pouch by tightly tying ends with string.

Soybeans and sausage are an extremely good combination, and, depending on the kind of sausage you use, can be very piquant. The following recipe has a definite Southern flavor, while the next two are perhaps the quickest for those in a hurry.

Soybeans and Sausage, Creole Style

1 pound pork sausage links, cut in quarters
½ cup chopped onion
½ cup chopped green peppers
1 clove garlic, minced
4 cups cooked soybeans, drained
2 8-ounce cans Spanish-style tomato sauce
¼ cup stock or water
1 teaspoon sugar
1 bay leaf, crumbled
    Tabasco sauce to taste
    Salt to taste

Preheat oven to 350° F.
Brown sausages in a skillet. Add onion, green peppers, and garlic. Cook until tender. Stir in beans, tomato sauce, stock or water, sugar, bay leaf, Tabasco sauce, and salt. Bring to a boil. Pour the bubbling mixture into a 2-quart casserole and bake in a preheated oven for 45 minutes.
    Serves 6.

The following group of recipes are all easy and quick to prepare—so they make ideal meals for the family. Not to be confused with authentic Mexican Chili Beans (see recipe on page 22), this is a Texas-style variation and is a family favorite.

Quick Chili Beans

3 or 4 tablespoons vegetable oil
1 cup chopped onion
2 or 3 cloves garlic, minced
2 teaspoons chili powder (or to taste)
1 can condensed cream of tomato soup (mixed with an
    equal amount of milk or water)
4 cups cooked soybeans, drained
¼ teaspoon cayenne (or to taste)
½ teaspoon oregano
    Salt to taste

Sauté onion in oil until tender. Add garlic and chili powder. Stir in tomato soup mixture, soybeans, cayenne, oregano, and salt.

Cover and simmer over low flame for 15 to 20 minutes. Stir frequently.

Serves 4 to 6.

Chili Beans and Franks

1 pound dried soybeans
2 bay leaves
2 cups tomatoes, mashed
3 carrots, chopped
3 medium onions, chopped
1 tablespoon chili powder (or to taste)
2 tablespoons dry mustard
2 or 3 tablespoons catsup
1 pound frankfurters, sliced
    Salt and freshly ground black pepper to taste

Prepare and cook beans (with 2 bay leaves) until tender, using any one of the basic recipes.

Add all other ingredients. Mix well and simmer about 30 minutes.

Serves 8 to 10.

Quick Baked Soybeans with Pepperoni

6 cups cooked soybeans, drained
2 medium onions, coarsely chopped
3 tablespoons olive oil
½ cup chili sauce
3 tablespoons molasses (blackstrap)
½ tablespoon dry mustard
¼ teaspoon dried basil
¾ cup red wine
½ pound pepperoni, sliced

Mix all ingredients well and cook in uncovered bean pot or deep greased casserole for 1 hour at 350°F.

Serves 6 to 8.

Beef and Soybean Skillet

1 pound ground beef
1 clove garlic, minced
2 tablespoons cornstarch
1 tablespoon sugar
4 tablespoons soy sauce
2 teaspoons horseradish
½ cup water
Tabasco sauce to taste
2½ cups cooked soybeans, drained

Slowly brown ground beef in a heavy skillet, breaking up lumps with a fork. Meanwhile, combine garlic, corn- starch, sugar, soy sauce, horseradish, water, and Tabasco. Mix well. When meat is cooked, add sauce to it and cook until mixture thickens. Then add beans and heat thoroughly.

Serves 4 to 6.

Sausage with Soybeans

4 large or 8 medium pork sausages
3 tablespoons olive oil
2 cups cooked soybeans
Salt and freshly ground black pepper to taste

Prick sausages with fork so they will not burst. Broil them until done. Fry soybeans in olive oil, stirring to avoid burning. Add seasonings. Serve in warm platter with broiled sausages on top.

Serves 2 to 3.

Variation: Fry the sausages slowly in a skillet. When done, remove, and fry the beans quickly in the sausage drippings. Serve beans topped with sausages.

2

❧ ❀ ❧

The Versatility of Soy Granules

Soy granules, or grits, cook quickly and blend in perfectly with whatever they are mixed with, thus lending themselves beautifully to the role of "meat extender" or "meat substitute"—truly a saving these days. For example, 1 cup of granules—costing only pennies—can "stretch" 1 pound of ground beef, normally serving 3 people, to make 6 hearty servings. It is not merely a bland filler, such as bread crumbs or rice, but is equally nutritious in its own right. In fact, a cup of granules is superior in food value in many ways to the meat that it is "extending." Just 1 tablespoon of granules adds an extra 6 grams of protein to any dish. It's difficult to go wrong with these kinds of advantages *once* you know.

Here's the best way to handle the granules.

Soy granules can take the place of about 20 to 25 percent of the meat in most ground-meat recipes.

As a "booster," try adding soy granules to almost any soup (canned or homemade)—1 tablespoon granules to each cup of soup. Soy granules can be used in place of rice or noodles in chicken and beef soups.

Don't forget that the granules—like rice or barley—will absorb liquid as they cook. Adding too many granules will make a dish dry (unless, of course, extra liquid is added too). An excellent and convenient solution is to prepare the granules beforehand: Add 1 cup boiling water (or milk) to 1 cup soy granules.

If you want a softer texture, put in a saucepan and cook gently for a few minutes. Allow to cool. Store in a tightly covered jar and refrigerate. This mixture can be added to scrambled eggs, soufflés, omelets, casseroles, croquettes, meat loaves, stuffings, etc. And you will doubtless find many more ways of using this marvelous preparation.

The following recipes represent a variety of dishes that illustrate the real versatility of soy granules.

Soyburgers Supreme

¾ cup milk
¾ cup soy granules
1 cup sour cream
1 envelope (1½ ounces) onion soup mix
Freshly ground black pepper to taste
1 pound ground beef

Mix milk with the soy granules. Then add sour cream, onion mix, and pepper. Add to ground beef and mix well. Shape into 6 or 8 patties and broil or grill to desired doneness (about 10 to 15 minutes).

Serves 6 to 8.

Meatballs

¼ cup soy granules
⅓ cup catsup
½ pound ground beef
¼ cup seasoned Italian bread crumbs
2 tablespoons parsley, minced
2 tablespoons minced onion
1½ teaspoons salt
   Freshly ground black pepper to taste

Mix granules with the catsup. Add all the other ingredients, mix well, and form into small balls. Fry slowly in a little fat until lightly browned. Serve. Makes 6-8 meatballs.

Variation: Put the cooked meatballs into a baking dish with cooked macaroni. Add your favorite tomato sauce and bake at 350° F. for about 20 minutes, or until bubbly and browned on top.

A variation for meatballs that is hard to beat for the right occasion!

Teriyaki Meatballs

½ cup soy granules
½ cup water or milk
1 tablespoon soy sauce
1 tablespoon water
2 teaspoons sugar
1 teaspoon grated onion
¼ teaspoon finely minced garlic
   Dash of MSG
   Dash of ground ginger
½ pound lean ground beef
   Vegetable oil for frying
   Hot rice to serve

Add water to granules, mix well, and let stand.

Combine soy sauce, water, sugar, grated onion, garlic, MSG, and ginger. Let stand 10 minutes. Combine ground meat and soy sauce mixture and mix well. Add soy granules and mix thoroughly. With the hands shape into ¾-inch meatballs. Fry in hot oil until well browned—this will take only 4 or 5 minutes. Makes about 2 dozen.

Serve immediately on a bed of hot rice, and sprinkle liberally with soy sauce.

Serves 2 to 3.

Salmon Loaf

2 cups cooked or canned salmon
1 cup soy granules
½ teaspoon salt
¼ teaspoon freshly ground black pepper
1 or 2 tablespoons grated onion
¾ cup milk
1 egg, slightly beaten
1 tablespoon lemon juice
  Butter
2 tablespoons parsley, minced (optional)
  Tomato sauce (optional)

Put salmon (and liquid), soy granules, and seasoning in a bowl and mix well. Add milk and egg, and gently but thoroughly mix. Stir in lemon juice and turn mixture into buttered loaf pan. Dot with butter and bake in 375° F. oven for 25 to 30 minutes, or until lightly browned. Serve plain, garnished with parsley, or with tomato sauce.

Serves 6 to 8.

Sausage with Soy Granules

½ pound uncooked pork sausage meat
¼ cup soy granules or soy flour

Mix together well, shape into patties, and fry slowly until well done.
Serves 6.

Chicken Croquettes

1½ cups leftover chicken (or turkey)
½ cup soy granules
¾ cup light cream
2 tablespoons melted butter
Salt and freshly ground black pepper to taste

Remove skin and bones from leftover chicken (or turkey) and pass through food grinder. You should have enough to make 1½ cups of ground meat. Soak the granules in the cream for 10 or 15 minutes. Mash smooth and blend into the chicken. Add melted butter and salt and pepper. Shape into 6 croquettes, and sauté in butter until browned on all sides.

Serve plain—or try these with Hollandaise sauce.

Chicken Hash

1 3-pound chicken
1 bay leaf
¼ pound butter
½ cup flour
2 or 3 large onions, chopped
4 stalks celery, chopped
2 or 3 cloves garlic, chopped
Salt and freshly ground black pepper to taste
Worcestershire sauce to taste
Red pepper to taste
6 scallions, including tops, chopped
¼ cup chopped parsley
1 cup soy granules
2 quarts stock

Boil chicken with bay leaf in a Dutch oven or large saucepan. Reserve the stock, then bone and chop meat into small pieces.

Melt butter in a heavy pan, and stir in flour until it is a smooth paste. Gradually add stock, stirring constantly, and heat to boiling. Add onions, celery, and garlic; season with salt, pepper, red pepper, and Worcestershire sauce. Simmer for 30 minutes. Add chicken meat, scallions, and parsley, cover, and simmer 20 minutes longer. Stir in soy granules and continue cooking, stirring continuously, until mixture thickens to consistency of hash.

Serves 6 to 8.

Codfish Patties

½ pound dried codfish
1½ cups cooked mashed potatoes
½ cup soy granules
½ cup milk
2 eggs, beaten
Flour
Cooking fat

Soak the codfish overnight in a saucepan. Drain, add fresh cold water. Bring to a boil and simmer until fish is tender. Drain fish and squeeze out all liquid. Shred the fish and remove any bones or skin.

Mix the fish with the mashed potatoes. Then, stir milk into the soy granules and add to fish and potatoes. Add eggs and mix well. Make into patties, dip lightly in flour, and fry in a little fat until golden brown on both sides.

Makes 6.

Eggplant Croquettes à la Diana

2 large eggplants
1 cup soy granules
4 tablespoons grated Parmesan cheese
1 tablespoon fresh parsley, minced, or 1 teaspoon dried parsley
1 tablespoon fresh basil, minced, or 1 teaspoon dried basil
1½ teaspoons salt
½ teaspoon freshly ground black pepper (or to taste)
Dash of nutmeg
2 eggs, beaten
½ cup flour
1 cup olive oil
Tomato sauce (optional)

Cut each eggplant into 6 or 8 slices and boil for 20 minutes, or until tender. Drain well and cut into small, fine pieces. Add soy granules and mix well. Mix in all the remaining ingredients (except the olive oil) and stir thoroughly. Shape into croquettes (or patties), flour well, and fry in olive oil until golden brown on both sides. Serve plain or with tomato sauce.

Makes 10 to 12.

Potato Soup

5 cups diced raw potatoes
4 thin slices onion
3 cups boiling water
½ cup soy granules
4 teaspoons salt (or to taste)
3 cups milk
1 tablespoon butter
   Pinch of thyme
¼ cup chopped parsley

Cook the potatoes and onion in the boiling water until soft. The water should be boiled down until there is approximately 2 cups. Put the potatoes and onion through a sieve or in the blender. Mix the soy granules with ½ cup of the potato liquid. Then add the rest of the ingredients (except parsley) and the potatoe purée and bring to a boil. Stir in the parsley and serve at once.

Serves 8.

Hearty Vegetable Soup

4 tablespoons butter
1 cup diced carrots
1 cup diced celery
1 cup diced cabbage
1 cup diced green peppers
2 cups diced potatoes
2 medium onions, chopped
8 cups chicken or beef stock
1 can tomatoes
1 cup soy granules
1 teaspoon salt (or to taste)
1 teaspoon marjoram

In a large heavy pan sauté all fresh vegetables in butter for about 10 minutes. Add stock, then the canned tomatoes. Cover and simmer for 30 minutes.

Add soy granules, salt, and marjoram, and stir in well. Simmer for 15 or 20 minutes more.

Serves 8 to 10.

Here's an unusual variation on a familiar dish. Soy granules make an excellent and healthful coating for broiled chicken and actually taste better than regular bread crumbs.

Batter for Broiled Chicken

In a flat pan blend 1 egg into 1 cup milk.

Salt and pepper each chicken piece and dip it into the egg and milk mixture, then dip it into another flat pan with soy granules.

Repeat with each piece. Broil until done.

If you prefer, skin the chicken before preparing.

Stuffed Cabbage

1 cup milk
1 cup soy granules
½ pound ground beef ⎫ OR 1 pound of any combination
½ pound ground pork ⎭   of ground meat
1 egg
1 teaspoon salt
Freshly ground black pepper to taste
1 teaspoon Worcestershire sauce
½ cup finely chopped onion
6 or 8 large cabbage leaves
1 10-¾-ounce can condensed tomato soup
2 tablespoons honey
1 tablespoon lemon juice

Preheat oven to 350° F. Mix together milk, granules, and ground meat and let stand. In a mixing bowl, combine egg, salt, pepper, Worcestershire sauce, and onion. Mix well. Blend with the ground meat and soy granule mixture, and mix together well.

Meanwhile, boil water and immerse cabbage leaves for about 3 minutes, or until just limp. Drain. The tough center vein may be slit about 2 inches from the bottom if necessary. Divide meat filling into 6 or 8 portions and place one on each cabbage leaf. Fold in sides and roll ends over meat so that filling is completely enveloped. Place in a 12-by-7½-inch baking dish.

Blend tomato soup, honey, and lemon juice; then pour over stuffed cabbage. Bake in a preheated oven for 1 hour and 15 minutes. Baste once or twice with the sauce.

Serves 6 or 8.

Basic Soy-Kasha

1 cup buckwheat groats (fine, medium, or coarse)
½ cup soy granules
1 egg, beaten
2½ cups boiling water
1½ teaspoons salt
Melted butter

Mix groats, granules, and egg with a fork in a saucepan over low heat until grains separate. Add the water and salt. Cover and cook over low heat for 15 minutes. Water should be completely absorbed.

Serve with melted butter.

Variation: Sauté chopped scallions, green peppers, or mushrooms in butter and stir into the cooked kasha.

Serves 3 to 4.

Soy-Kasha Poultry Stuffing

(per 5 pounds of meat)

Start with the basic soy-kasha recipe. While it is cooking, dice 1 large onion, ½ cup celery, and 1 tart apple. Sauté them in oil and add to the soy-kasha-egg mixture before adding boiling water. Add 1 to 2 teaspoons poultry seasoning and freshly ground black pepper to taste. Use as you would regular stuffing.

Soy-Kasha Stuffing for Roast Lamb Shoulder

Follow the same steps as above; however, sauté 1 clove garlic, minced, along with the onion and celery.

This versatile recipe is good as a side dish, or alternatively makes an ideal meat substitute.

Soy Pilaf

2 cups (or 1 13-¾-ounce can) chicken broth
1¼ cups soy granules
1 egg, beaten
¾ cup chopped onion
¼ cup butter
Salt and freshly ground black pepper to taste

Heat chicken broth and add soy granules. Mix well and stir in the beaten egg. Sauté onion in butter, and add to soy granule mixture. Salt and pepper to taste. Mix well so that it has a fluffy consistency.

Serves 3 or 4.

Soy Polenta

    1 cup cornmeal
    ⅓ cup soy granules
    5 cups water
    2 tablespoons butter
    3 tablespoons grated Parmesan or Romano cheese
      Salt to taste
      Butter for frying
      Tomato sauce (optional)

Mix cornmeal and soy granules, and then gradually add to 5 cups boiling water in the saucepan. Stir constantly to prevent lumping and sticking to the pan. The water may be absorbed quickly, so watch carefully. Continue stirring and add butter, grated cheese, and salt. Pour into a wet glass baking dish (about 8-by-12 inches). Let cool and chill.

Then remove from fridge and cut into small squares or triangles. Fry in sizzling hot butter (on both sides). Put pieces back in baking dish, sprinkle with grated cheese, and bake in 350° F. oven until cheese browns. Serve plain or with your favorite tomato sauce.

Serves 4.

Omelet

    4 egg yolks
    ¼ cup soy granules
    ¼ cup milk
    1 tablespoon chives, finely minced
    1 tablespoon parsley, finely minced
    4 egg whites
    ½ teaspoon salt
    ¼ cup water
    1 tablespoon butter

Preheat oven to 300° F.

Separate the eggs, and beat the egg yolks until creamy. Mix soy granules with milk and blend with egg yolks. Add chives and parsley and mix well. In another bowl mix egg whites, water, and salt, and beat until stiff. Fold the egg yolk mixture gradually into the whites. Pour into a frying pan containing melted butter. Cover and cook slowly over low heat until set around the edge. Remove cover and put skillet in a preheated oven for 15 or 20 minutes, or until omelet is done and lightly browned on top. Sprinkle with grated cheese if you like, and fold over. Serve at once.

Serves 3 or 4.

Potato Patties

    1 egg, beaten
    ¼ cup soy granules
    2 cups cooked mashed potatoes
      Salt and freshly ground black pepper to taste

Mix beaten egg and soy granules. Add mashed potatoes and seasoning and mix together well. Shape into patties, dip lightly in flour, and fry in oil until golden brown. Serve immediately.

Makes 6.

3

✳ ❀ ✳

Soups and Stews

This classic Italian dish is really more of a casserole than a soup. But I'm including it here, because it is really versatile and you can keep it for a day or two in the fridge. If you are *not* familiar with it, you are in for a great treat.

Minestra di Pasta e Fagiòli
(Macaroni and Bean Soup)

1 pound dried soybeans
2 cups chopped celery
1 large onion, coarsely chopped
2 cloves garlic, chopped
2 carrots, chopped
1 28-ounce can tomatoes, mashed
½ pound tubettina (macaroni)
6 tablespoons olive oil
   Salt and freshly ground black pepper to taste
¾ cup freshly grated Romano cheese

Prepare and cook the beans by any one of the three basic methods. When the beans are tender, add the celery, onion, garlic, carrots, and tomatoes. Simmer for 15 minutes. If the liquid has cooked down to a level below the vegetables, add another 1 to 2 cups water; bring mixture to a boil. Add tubettina and reduce to simmer. As the macaroni cooks, it will absorb liquid, so watch that the mixture does not become dry. Add more water as necessary. When the tubettina is cooked, add the oil and salt and pepper. Sprinkle with the grated cheese. Serve piping hot.

Serves 8 to 10.

Variation: The pasta may be cooked separately according to the directions on the package, and then added to the rest of the ingredients, which have already been cooked according to the recipe.

This version uses precooked beans and macaroni.

Quick and Easy Pasta e Fagiòli

1 medium onion, coarsely chopped
1 clove garlic, minced
4 tablespoons olive oil
1 15-ounce can tomatoes, mashed
1 carrot, chopped
1 cup chopped celery
1 to 2 cups stock or bouillon (depending on desired thickness of soup)
3 cups cooked soybeans, drained
2 cups cooked tubettina, drained
  Freshly ground black pepper and salt to taste
  Freshly grated Romano cheese

Sauté onion and garlic in oil. When transparent, add tomatoes, carrot, celery, and stock. Simmer for 15 minutes, or until vegetables are tender. Add the soybeans and tubettina. Heat thoroughly on low heat. Salt and pepper to taste. Serve piping hot, and sprinkle generously with freshly grated cheese.

Serves 4 to 6.

The secret of a good stew is to cook all ingredients until tender, but not to overcook any ingredient.

Hearty Beef and Soybean Stew

 1 pound dried soybeans
 2 bay leaves
 2 pounds stew beef, cut into 1-inch cubes
 1 28-ounce can tomatoes, mashed
 5 or 6 small carrots, sliced
10 small whole onions
 3 or 4 cloves garlic, chopped
 1 tablespoon chili powder
 1 teaspoon oregano
   Salt and freshly ground black pepper to taste
 2 green peppers, sliced
 3 stalks celery, chopped

Cook the beans, along with 2 bay leaves, until tender, using any one of the basic recipes. Add the beef and cook until tender (about 1 hour). Add tomatoes, carrots, onions, garlic, and other seasonings (chili powder, oregano, salt, and pepper). Cook this for 15 minutes until carrots and onions are tender, add celery and green peppers and cook for about another 10 minutes, until done.

Serves 8 to 10.

Soybean Soup

1 pound dried soybeans
1 bay leaf
2 onions, coarsely chopped
2 carrots, coarsely chopped
1 celery stalk, chopped
¼ teaspoon thyme
1 cup scalded milk
   Salt and freshly ground black pepper to taste
3 tablespoons butter

Prepare and cook soybeans (with bay leaf), using basic recipe, until very tender. Add onions, carrots, celery, and thyme. Cook together until tender. Drain, reserving liquid. Make purée of vegetables by running through food grinder or mixing in the blender. Return to pot and add milk. Stir in cooking liquid until desired soup consistency is reached. (If more liquid is needed, add stock or water, a little at a time). Bring soup to boiling point but do not allow to boil. Add salt and pepper to taste. Take off the heat and add butter, stirring until it is melted and well blended.
   Serves 6.

This makes a good dish for winter evenings, or a Sunday night supper around the fire.

Spanish Soybean Soup

1 pound dried soybeans
1 large cabbage, chopped
1 ham hock or ¼ pound ham, cubed
1 or 2 onions, chopped
½ teaspoon or more crushed red pepper
1 or 2 cloves garlic, chopped
  Salt to taste

Prepare beans according to the freezer method (see page 11). Simmer for 1½ or 2 hours. Add all the other ingredients, cover, and continue simmering until beans are tender—about 2 more hours.
Serves 8.

East African Soybean Soup

2 cups cooked soybeans, drained
1 large ripe tomato, chopped
1 large onion, chopped
1 green pepper, seeded and chopped
2 cups coconut milk
1 teaspoon curry powder
  Salt to taste

Put all ingredients in saucepan and bring to a boil. Reduce the heat, cover, and simmer for about 20 minutes, or until mixture is thick. Stir well before serving. It should have the consistency of thin purée, with the beans still visible.
Serves 4.

Japanese Soybean Soup

2 cups cooked soybeans, drained
2 tablespoons vinegar
2 tablespoons beer
5 cups beef stock
¼ pound raw shrimp, shelled, deveined, and chopped
½ cup grated turnip
1 cup grated carrots
4 eggs, beaten
2 tablespoons soy sauce
½ cup chopped scallions

Purée beans in a food grinder, force through colander, or purée in a blender. (If using a blender, first add vinegar, beer, and enough beef stock to facilitate blending.) Mix with vinegar and beer.

Bring the stock to a boil and add the prepared shrimps, turnips, and carrots. Simmer for 10 minutes. Then stir in bean mixture, making sure it is well blended in. Simmer for about 5 minutes more.

Mix together eggs, soy sauce, and scallions. Stir into the soup and continue stirring until eggs set.

Serves 6 to 8.

Soybean and Cabbage Soup

4 pounds cabbage, shredded
2 medium onions, chopped
4 tablespoons butter
. 3 tablespoons flour
5 cups water
2 cups cooked soybeans, drained
2 cups canned tomatoes, mashed
2 teaspoons salt, or to taste
½ teaspoon freshly ground black pepper, or to taste
2 tablespoons sugar
3 tablespoons lemon juice
1 teaspoon caraway seeds
   Sour cream

Cook the cabbage and onion in butter for about 15 minutes. Sprinkle with flour and gradually add water, about a cup at a time. Stir frequently until mixture reaches the boiling point. Add beans, tomatoes, salt, pepper, sugar, lemon juice, and caraway seeds. Blend gently together.

Cover and simmer for about 1 hour. Garnish each serving with a spoonful of sour cream.

Serves 8.

Here's another simple but satisfying soup for cold days.

Rice and Soybean Soup

⅓ cup vegetable oil
1 medium onion, chopped
2 cloves garlic, minced
3 cups cooked soybeans, drained
½ cup bean stock or water
2 cups cooked rice
1 13-¾-ounce can beef broth
¼ teaspoon cayenne
  Salt to taste

Heat oil in heavy saucepan; sauté onion and garlic until transparent. Add beans and stock or water and simmer 5 to 10 minutes. Purée in blender or colander. Pour back into saucepan and add cooked rice, beef broth, and cayenne. Salt to taste and simmer for 5 minutes more.
  Serves 4 to 6.

While not strictly soup, this makes a great party appetizer. Serve it with carrot strips, celery, and cauliflower segments.

Soybean Dip

2 cups cooked soybeans, drained
⅔ cup tahini (sesame butter)
¾ cup lemon juice
2 cloves garlic
1 teaspoon salt
  Chopped parsley for garnish

Place all ingredients except parsley in a blender and blend until smooth. Garnish and serve.
  Makes about 3 cups.

4

❧ ✿ ❧

Salads

Bean salads are definitely welcome any time of the year. But in the hot summer months, when most of us lose interest in heavy, rich foods, they are a special attraction. This is also the time when good fresh vegetables (and fresh herbs) are in abundance, and they should be used whenever possible.

Soybeans, with their high protein content, are ideal for any bean salad. When combined with fresh vegetables, they can create a complete one-dish meal. So you save time as well as dollars and cents. Most of these salads are just as good—or even better—on the second day, so double (or triple) your favorite recipes and relax a bit.

Since bean salads are made with precooked beans, you will find it very practical to cook 2 or 3 pounds of beans at one time, and store what you're not using immediately in the refrigerator or freezer. It is so convenient to have them on hand—cooked and ready—for these and other recipes.

One of the first recipes I learned to make was a dish my mother prepared often, especially in the summer. At that time we called the dish simply "bean salad," but I shall rename it:

Soybeans à la Nell

4 cups cooked soybeans, drained
2 good-sized tomatoes, coarsely chopped
1 green pepper, chopped
1 medium small onion, sliced very fine, or 3 or 4 chopped scallions
1 tablespoon prepared mustard
3 tablespoons catsup
½ cup prepared salad dressing
Freshly ground black pepper and salt to taste

Simply mix all the ingredients and chill well. As a variation add 1 cup chopped celery.

Serves 4 to 6.

Simple Soybean Salad

2 cups cooked soybeans, drained
1 clove garlic, finely minced
¼ cup onion, finely sliced
1 ripe tomato, coarsely chopped
¼ cup parsley, finely chopped
½ cup olive oil
2 or 3 tablespoons wine vinegar
Salt and freshly ground black pepper to taste

Put all the vegetables in a salad bowl. Add salt and pepper, vinegar and oil, and toss. May be chilled or served immediately at room temperature.
Serves 2.

This is an easy salad too, which looks as attractive as it tastes.

Tangy Soybean Salad

2 cups cooked soybeans, drained
¼ cup chopped pimiento
½ cup chopped green pepper
1 cup chopped celery
½ to ¾ cup mayonnaise or salad dressing
2 tablespoons or more prepared horseradish
Salt and freshly ground black pepper to taste
Lettuce leaves to serve

Blend mayonnaise and horseradish. Place all the vegetables in a mixing bowl; pour the dressing over them and toss until well mixed.
Serve on crisp lettuce leaves.
Serves 4 to 6.

Soybean Remoulade

2 cups cooked soybeans, drained
2 anchovy fillets, chopped
1 clove garlic, finely minced
1 green onion, finely chopped
1 tablespoon capers, finely chopped
2 tablespoons parsley, finely chopped
⅓ to ½ cup mayonnaise
   Lemon juice to taste
   Freshly ground black pepper and salt to taste

Mix all ingredients together in a large bowl and chill.
Serves 2.

Soybeans Vinaigrette

5 cups cooked soybeans, cooled and drained
Dressing:
½ cup olive oil
½ cup tarragon vinegar
1 teaspoon salt
½ teaspoon freshly ground black pepper
2 teaspoons minced chives
3 teaspoons minced capers
2 hard-boiled eggs, minced
½ teaspoon dry mustard
⅛ teaspoon dried chervil

Mix all ingredients for dressing thoroughly and pour
over soybeans. This may be served immediately, but is best
when allowed to marinate a few hours in refrigerator before
serving. Stir occasionally before serving.
Serves 5 to 6.

Soybeans aux Fines Herbes

4 cups cooked soybeans, cooled and drained

Dressing:

⅔ cup olive oil
½ cup wine vinegar
¼ cup dry white wine
1½ teaspoons salt
½ teaspoon freshly ground black pepper
½ teaspoon dry mustard
½ teaspoon dried basil
½ cup chopped parsley
1 clove garlic, minced

Blend all dressing ingredients until smooth. Pour over beans and let stand a few hours in refrigerator before serving. Stir occasionally.

Serves 4.

Soybean and Tuna Salad

4 cups cooked soybeans, drained
1 10-ounce can tuna packed in water, flaked
½ cup onion, finely chopped
Salt and freshly ground black pepper to taste
½ cup olive oil
3 tablespoons fresh lemon juice
Hard-boiled eggs and finely chopped parsley to garnish (optional)

In a bowl, mix beans, tuna, and onions. Add salt and pepper. Pour on oil and lemon juice, and mix well. Set aside for an hour or so at room temperature. This salad may be garnished with sliced hard-boiled eggs and finely chopped parsley.

Serves 4 to 6.

Soybean Salad Niçoise

5 tablespoons olive oil
2 tablespoons vinegar
1 tablespoon capers, minced
1 teaspoon oregano
   Salt and freshly ground black pepper to taste
3 cups cooked soybeans, drained
3 tomatoes, sliced
1 medium onion, thinly sliced
3 hard-boiled eggs, sliced
8 anchovy fillets

Pour oil into a cup or mixing jar. Add vinegar, capers, oregano, salt and pepper; mix well. Put beans in a salad bowl, then one layer of tomato slices, one layer of onions, and one layer of sliced eggs. Pour dressing over salad and garnish with anchovy fillets.
   Serves 4.

Soybean and Egg Salad with French Dressing

4 cups cooked soybeans, drained
1 cup celery, chopped fine
½ cup sweet pickle relish
4 hard-boiled eggs, chopped
4 tablespoons onion, minced
   Lettuce leaves to serve

Dressing:
4 tablespoons vinegar or lemon juice
½ cup olive oil or salad oil
1 or 2 cloves garlic, minced
   Salt and freshly ground black pepper to taste

Mix together all the ingredients for dressing in a small jar or cup. Put the soybeans, celery, relish, hard-boiled eggs, and onion in a mixing bowl, toss lightly, and pour on the dressing. Mix together well and chill. Serve on crisp lettuce leaves.
Serves 4 to 6.

Soybean and Egg Salad

4 cups cooked soybeans, drained
4 hard-boiled eggs, chopped
¼ cup onion, finely chopped
½ cup mayonnaise
1 tablespoon prepared mustard
3 tablespoons catsup
   Salt and freshly ground black pepper to taste
4 slices bacon (fried crisp, drained, and crumbled)
   Lettuce leaves to serve

Combine beans, eggs, and onion in a bowl. Chill. Meanwhile blend mayonnaise, mustard, and catsup, and pour over bean mixture. Salt and pepper to taste. Toss together well and serve over crisp lettuce leaves. Sprinkle with bacon bits.
Serves 4.

Another dish that is as attractive as it is tasty—and perfect for special lunches.

Soybean Salad-Cake

> 3 cups cooked soybeans, drained and firmly packed
> 1 tablespoon grated onion
> 1 teaspoon sugar
> 1 teaspoon salt (or to taste)
> 6 tablespoons lemon juice
> 3 tablespoons vegetable oil
> 2 tablespoons sour cream
> 1 bunch scallions including tops, chopped
> 2 tablespoons fresh dill, chopped
> 2 tablespoons parsley, chopped
> 6 black olives, pits removed
> 6 radish roses

Put first 7 ingredients in a blender and purée. (This can also be done by running cooked beans through a food grinder. Then add the other 6 ingredients and mix well.)

With a spatula turn mixture onto a serving plate and shape into a "cake" about 1-inch thick.

Garnish with chopped scallions, fresh dill, and parsley.

Place radish roses and olives on top so that when sliced, each cut will have one of each.

Serves 6.

Note: The bean purée makes a delicious dip for vegetables—or a stuffing for celery, cherry tomatoes, etc.

Soybean and Pimiento Salad

2 cups cooked soybeans, drained
2 tablespoons olive oil
2 tablespoons wine vinegar
1 tablespoon chopped parsley
2 chopped scallions, including tops
1 small jar pimientos, chopped
  Salt and freshly ground black pepper to taste

Combine all ingredients in a bowl and chill several hours before serving.
Serves 3 or 4.

Mexican Salad

2 cups cooked soybeans, drained
3 tablespoons lemon juice
1 tablespoon wine vinegar
¼ cup olive oil
1 tablespoon grated onions
1 tablespoon minced parsley
2 tablespoons bell pepper, chopped fine
1 cup celery, chopped
¼ teaspoon oregano
  Pinch of thyme
  Salt to taste

Mix all ingredients together in a bowl. Toss and chill at least 2 hours before serving.
Serves 2 or 3.

The success of this garden-fresh dish depends on the *fresh* parsley, dill, and mint. It could be made with dried herbs but would not be nearly as good.

Soybean Salad with Fresh Herbs

¼ cup olive oil
Juice of 1 lemon
Salt and freshly ground black pepper to taste
2 cups cooked soybeans, drained
4 scallions with tops, chopped
1 teaspoon each fresh parsley, dill, and mint, minced
1 tomato, quartered
1 hard-boiled egg, quartered

Mix oil, lemon juice, salt and pepper in a salad bowl. Add beans and scallions to the dressing and mix well. Sprinkle chopped parsley, dill, and mint on top; garnish with quartered tomato and egg.
Serves 2 to 4.

This very colorful dish is perfect for festive occasions, although the simplicity of preparation makes it even more attractive as an "everyday" dish.

Beet and Soybean Salad

1 16-ounce jar sliced, pickled beets (or sliced, pickled beets with onions), chopped
3 cups cooked soybeans, drained
1 cup sour cream
Dill, fresh or dried, as garnish

Drain off about half of liquid from beets. Combine beets, beans, and sour cream in a bowl. Toss together well. Let marinate at least 2 hours in refrigerator. Garnish with fresh or dried dill.

Serves 4 to 6.

Chilled Soybean Casserole

2 cups chopped onion
1 clove garlic, minced
¾ cup olive oil
2 tomatoes, chopped
¼ cup parsley, minced
5 cups cooked soybeans, drained
2 or 3 tablespoons wine vinegar
   Salt and freshly ground black pepper to taste
2 scallions, including tops, finely chopped

Sauté onion and garlic in ½ cup oil until tender. Add the chopped tomatoes and parsley and simmer, stirring frequently, for about 10 minutes.

Mix the beans with the cooked and cooled tomato mixture and chill well. Just before serving add remaining ¼ cup oil and the vinegar. Salt and pepper to taste. Garnish with chopped scallions.

Serves 6 to 8.

5

❧ ❀ ❧

Soybeans for the Family

The versatility of soybeans and soy granules is one of the delightful qualities of this most nutritious food staple. Offer them in any one of this panoply of serving ideas. Prepare precooked beans according to any one of the methods given on page 10; granules need no other forethought than to have them always on hand.

Soybean Surprise

2 cups cooked soybeans, drained
½ cup catsup
2 tablespoons vegetable oil
1 clove garlic, minced
1 4-ounce can mild green chilis, drained
1 teaspoon Worcestershire sauce
  Salt and freshly ground black pepper to taste
1 cup grated sharp Cheddar cheese
  Crisp bacon, crumbled (optional)
  Chips or crackers to serve

Combine all ingredients (except cheese and bacon) in a saucepan. Heat thoroughly until slightly bubbly. Pour into blender, add cheese, and blend (at high speed) until well blended. Pour into chafing dish and cover with crumbled bacon. Serve with chips or crackers.

Makes about 3 cups.

Refried beans is one of the most popular dishes in Mexican cuisine. This rather fancy soybean version may raise the purist's eyebrows, but it's so good it deserves to be known.

Refried Beans

1 medium onion, chopped
1 clove garlic, finely chopped
1 medium tomato, coarsely chopped
4 tablespoons bacon drippings
1 tablespoon chili powder
3 tablespoons tomato catsup
3 cups cooked soybeans, puréed in food grinder or colander
   Salt to taste

Sauté onion, garlic, and tomato in the bacon drippings until tender. Mash with a fork, until pulpy. Add chili powder and catsup, and cook together for about 5 minutes. Gradually add bean purée and continue stirring until mixture becomes creamy. Salt to taste.

Makes about 5 cups.

Refried beans may be served as a side dish (generously sprinkled with grated cheese) or with tortillas. One typical Mexican dish using refried beans and tortillas is called:

Burritos

Warm the tortillas (preferably "flour tortillas," although "corn tortillas" will do) in a skillet or on a griddle. Spread with refried beans and roll up. Serve hot or cold. You may prefer buttering the hot tortilla before spreading it with the bean mixture.

The refried-bean recipe makes a delicious spread for sandwiches or crackers. It also makes an excellent stuffing for peppers, tomatoes, onions, or zucchini.

Stuffed Bell Peppers

3 large peppers (or 4 medium peppers)
  Refried-bean recipe (see recipe on page 72)
2 8-ounce cans Spanish-style tomato sauce
2 cups grated sharp Cheddar cheese
  Hot rice to serve

Preheat oven to 400° F.

Wash peppers and cut in half (lengthwise). Remove seeds. Fill with bean mixture. Put into a greased baking dish. Heat the tomato sauce in a saucepan and pour over the peppers, then bake in a preheated oven for about an hour, or until peppers are tender. When done, remove from oven and sprinkle a generous amount of grated cheese over each stuffed pepper. Return to oven for another 5 minutes. The peppers may be served on a bed of rice with the remaining sauce over them.

Serves 6 or 8.

Variation: Mix the remaining sauce with the rice before making individual servings.

This does equally well as an appetizer or as a side dish with the main meal.

Armenian Soybeans

3 cups cooked soybeans, drained
1 cup stock
3 tablespoons olive oil
1 carrot, sliced
2 stalks celery, sliced
2 tablespoons parsley, chopped
1 tablespoon fresh dill, chopped
2 cloves garlic, minced
    Salt and freshly ground black pepper to taste
    Lemon wedges

Sauté carrot and celery in olive oil, and add parsley, dill, and garlic. Cook until garlic turns pale yellow. Pour in beans, stock, and salt and pepper, and simmer for about 15 minutes. Serve at room temperature with lemon wedges. As a side dish serves 3 or 4. As an appetizer, serves 10.

Another tasty appetizer, also of Middle Eastern origin—this one comes from Egypt.

Soybean Appetizer

1 cup cooked soybeans, drained
½ teaspoon salt (or to taste)
¼ cup olive oil
2 tablespoons lemon juice
1 scallion, minced
1 small clove garlic, finely minced
   Lettuce leaves
   Scallions to garnish

Mix all ingredients together and chill. Stir occasionally.
Serve on lettuce leaves garnished with scallions.
   Makes 4 small servings.

Hot Sausage Soybean Dip

½ pound pork sausage
2 cups cooked soybeans, drained
½ cup sharp Cheddar cheese, grated
3 tablespoons catsup
½ teaspoon prepared mustard
   Hot pepper sauce to taste
   Crackers or corn chips to serve

Chop up sausage and slowly brown in skillet. Drain off
most of fat. Put sausage and all other ingredients into a
blender and blend until creamy. Reheat in skillet and serve
with crackers or corn chips.
   Makes 4 cups.

These "franks" are easy to make, and if you have a large family they are very cheap in cost per serving. Try them in frankfurter buns with your favorite relish. They are ideal for your child's lunch box, or as a snack.

Soybean "Franks"

1 pound soybeans, soaked, drained, and frozen
1¼ cup catsup
2 or 3 garlic cloves, finely minced
1¼ cups bread crumbs
2 eggs
1½ teaspoons chili powder
1½ teaspoons sage
1 teaspoon oregano
1 teaspoon cumin
1½ teaspoons salt
½ teaspoon freshly ground black pepper
Oil for deep frying

Grind the soaked and frozen beans in a food grinder (use medium blade) or a blender. Mix in all other ingredients. Shape into "sausages" approximately 3 to 4 inches long and 1 inch thick. Chill for an hour or so. Using a spatula, carefully ease into hot oil (375° F.). Fry until nicely browned. Drain. Serve with mustard or catsup.

Makes about 20.

Soybean Loaf #1

2 cups cooked soybeans, drained and firmly packed
1 onion, finely chopped
1 green pepper, finely chopped
4 eggs, beaten
1½ cups milk
5 tablespoons butter, melted
5 tablespoons bread crumbs
1 tablespoons parsley, finely chopped
4 tablespoons grated cheese
⅛ teaspoon nutmeg
Salt and freshly ground black pepper to taste

Purée beans and mix well with all other ingredients.*
Pour into a greased loaf pan (9¼-by-5¼-by-2¾ inches)
and set the loaf pan in a larger pan containing water; water
should come up to halfway level on loaf pan. Bake in a
moderate oven (350° to 375° F.) until mixture is good and
firm (about 1½ hours). Serve immediately.
Serves 4 to 6.

* *Blender method*: Blend beans in milk. Add beaten eggs and
all other ingredients. Follow above instructions for baking.

This dish should really be named "Mock Lasagna." Everyone who tries it comments on the similarity.

Soybean Loaf #2 with Tomato Sauce

4 cups cooked soybeans, drained and firmly packed
2 tablespoons butter
1 onion, chopped
1 ripe tomato, chopped
4 eggs, beaten
5 tablespoons grated Parmesan cheese
1 cup Italian bread crumbs
1 tablespoon parsley, minced
1 teaspoon salt
  Tomato sauce
  Grated Parmesan cheese

Preheat oven between 325° and 350° F.

Purée soybeans in food grinder or colander. Sauté onion in butter. Add tomato and sauté until mushy, then mix this with the puréed soybeans. Add all other ingredients and mix thoroughly. Pour into greased baking dish (8-by-8 inches) and bake in a preheated oven for about 30 minutes, or until center is set. Cut into 6 squares and serve with tomato sauce and grated Parmesan cheese.

Serves 6.

This simple recipe is a quick and satisfying solution for lunch or supper. I suggest it for a cold winter day with Italian bread and a nice red wine.

Soybeans Luigi

2 cups cooked soybeans, drained
⅓ cup olive oil
Salt and freshly ground black pepper to taste
Oregano

Heat the beans in olive oil. Add salt and pepper, then sprinkle with oregano.

If you like, sauté a small onion or small clove of garlic in olive oil before adding beans.

Serves 2.

Soy-Pimiento Loaf

6 cups cooked soybeans, drained
3 tablespoons butter
1 cup chopped onion
2 eggs, beaten
½ cup minced pimiento
4 tablespoons minced parsley
1½ teaspoons salt
¼ teaspoons pepper
¼ teaspoon thyme

Preheat oven to 350° F.

Purée beans in a food mill or colander. Sauté onion in butter until limp. Add to bean purée. Add all other ingredients and mix thoroughly. Turn into a buttered loaf pan and bake in a preheated oven for 35 minutes.

Serves 6 to 8.

Now for a staple that will keep the family healthy *and* satisfied.

Simple Meat Loaf

¾ pound ground meat
1½ cups tomato juice or milk
2 or 3 slices bacon, fried crisp and crumbled
1 small onion, minced
1 stalk celery, chopped
¾ cup soy granules
2 tablespoons parsley, minced
2 teaspoons salt (or to taste)
¾ cup seasoned Italian bread crumbs
Freshly ground black pepper to taste

In a large bowl, mix meat with tomato juice or milk. Sauté the onion and celery in the fat from bacon for a few minutes. Add all the ingredients to the meat and mix together well.

Shape into loaf, place in uncovered pan, and bake at 350° F. until well done and brown, about 1 hour.

Serves 4-6.

Try this more sophisticated version, which has a very distinctive flavor.

Liver Loaf

¾ cup boiling chicken stock
¾ pound beef, lamb, or calves' liver
1 medium onion
½ pound pork sausage meat
1 tablespoon Worcestershire sauce
1 clove garlic, finely minced
½ cup finely chopped celery
2 eggs, beaten
⅛ teaspoon freshly ground black pepper (or to taste)
1½ teaspoons salt (or to taste)
1 cup soy granules
3 slices bacon

Preheat oven to 350° F.

Place liver in a saucepan, and over it pour boiling stock; simmer for 5 minutes. Remove liver and reserve stock for later.

Grind the liver and onion in a food grinder using medium knife. Add the stock with all the remaining ingredients except the bacon. Mix well and mold into a greased 1-quart loaf pan. Top with bacon and bake 45 minutes in a preheated oven.

Serves 6 to 8.

Here is a super-special meat loaf you will be proud to serve on any occasion.

Fancy Meat Loaf with Curry Stuffing

¾ cup soy granules
1 cup milk
2 pounds ground beef
3 slices uncooked bacon, chopped
2 tablespoons Worcestershire sauce
2 eggs
2 teaspoons salt
1 teaspoon dry mustard
½ teaspoon freshly ground black pepper
2 cloves garlic, minced
3 tablespoons parsley, minced

Preheat oven to 350° F.

Combine the soy granules and milk. Take ½ of this mixture and mix well with all other ingredients. Spread about ⅔ of the resultant mixture in an ungreased loaf pan (9 by 5 by 3 inches). Press mixture up sides of pan to within ¾ inch of top.

Now spread stuffing (recipe below) over this mixture and top with remaining ⅓ of meat mixture. Cover completely. Bake in a preheated oven for about 1 hour and 10 minutes. Drain off fat and let stand a few minutes before serving.

Serves 8.

Stuffing:
¼ cup butter
1 medium onion, chopped
1 cup chopped celery, with leaves
½ teaspoon salt
⅓ cup raisins
1 tablespoon curry powder
½ cup catsup

Melt butter in a large skillet. Add onion and celery, and sauté until onion is tender. Stir in other ingredients, including the remaining ½ of soy-granule mixture. Heat thoroughly before spreading on loaf mixture.

This tasty loaf uses soy granules (see Chapter 2) and is an excellent meat substitute.

Soy-Mushroom Loaf

1 cup soy granules
1 cup milk
1½ teaspoons salt
1 medium onion, chopped
1 or 2 cloves garlic, minced
¼ pound butter
1 pound fresh mushrooms (remove stems and chop)
2 eggs, beaten
¼ teaspoon dried dill

Preheat oven to 350° F.
Add milk and salt to soy granules. Mix well.
Sauté onion and garlic in butter until translucent. Add mushrooms and sauté until tender.
Remove from heat and add to the granule mixture. Mix

well. Add eggs and dill. Mix thoroughly. Pour into a 8-by-8-inch baking dish and bake in a preheated oven for 30 minutes. Cut into 4 portions and serve.

Serves 4.

I urge the reader to try this recipe no matter how skeptical he or she may be. You'll be surprised how much you like this Mexican treat.

Bean and Banana Fritters

    3 bananas
    5 tablespoons all-purpose flour
    ¼ teaspoon salt (or to taste)
    1 tablespoon lemon juice
    1 cup cooked soybeans, drained
    2 tablespoons oil for frying

Mash bananas, add flour, salt, and lemon juice. Mix well. Add beans and mix well together.

Heat oil in a skillet and spoon in mixture to make patties about 3 inches in diameter. Brown quickly on both sides.

Makes 6.

Soybean and Potato Patties

2 or 3 medium potatoes
1 or 2 tablespoons milk or cream
1 egg, beaten
  Salt and freshly ground black pepper to taste
1 cup cooked soybeans, drained
2 tablespoons vegetable oil for frying

Cook potatoes until tender. Mash with a fork and add milk, egg, and salt and pepper. Add beans, mix well, and shape into patties. Heat oil in a skillet and brown the patties on both sides.
Makes 6.

Soybean Croquettes

3 cups cooked soybeans, drained
¾ cup catsup
2 eggs
1 teaspoon salt
2 tablespoons finely chopped parsley
1 box (6 ounces) Bell's Stuffing
  Freshly ground black pepper to taste
  Vegetable oil for deep-frying

Purée beans in catsup. Add other ingredients and mix well. Shape with fingers into conical croquettes. Brown in a skillet or fry in deep fat (350° F.).
Makes 10 or 12.

Variation: Serve with your favorite tomato sauce or white sauce.

The West Africans eat these balls hot *or* cold. I've never tasted one cold, simply because there is never even one left over! But they're absolutely delicious. You can even make smaller-sized balls and serve them on toothpicks for a cocktail treat.

Soybean Balls

3 cups cooked beans, drained
1 egg, beaten
Salt to taste
1 medium onion, finely minced
1 small green pepper, finely minced
½ teaspoon red pepper (or to taste)
2 tablespoons flour
Vegetable oil for deep-frying

Purée beans in a food grinder or colander. Add egg and salt. Mix well. Then add onion, green pepper, red pepper, and flour. Mix until smooth. Let the mixture stand for at least ½ hour. Form into balls (or patties). The easiest method of doing this is to drop a lump of the soybean mixture (approximately the size of a golf ball) into a small bowl of flour. Spoon the flour over the bean mixture, covering it completely. Now it can easily be shaped into balls. Fry in oil heated to 350° to 375° F. until brown.

Makes about 1½ dozen.

Mexican Croquettes

2 cups cooked soybeans, drained and firmly packed
2 tablespoons chopped onion
½ teaspoon oregano
1 4-ounce can peeled mild green chilis, drained and
   chopped
4 tablespoons grated Parmesan cheese
   Salt to taste
¼ pound Cheddar cheese, cut into 6 or 8 pieces
   Bread crumbs
1 egg, beaten with 1 tablespoon water
   Vegetable oil for deep-frying

Run soybeans through a food grinder or mash well with a fork. Combine with onion, oregano, chopped chilis, Parmesan cheese, and salt. Mix well and form into croquettes, inserting a small piece of Cheddar cheese into the center of each. Be sure cheese is completely covered with bean mixture. Roll in bread crumbs, then in beaten egg, and roll again in bread crumbs. Fry in deep fat until brown. Serve alone or with chili sauce.

Makes 6 to 8 croquettes.

Spanish Omelet with Soybeans #1

2 tablespoons olive oil
¾ cup cooked soybeans, drained
2 eggs, beaten
Salt to taste

Heat olive oil and fry beans lightly; remove from heat. Allow to cool at least 5 minutes. Add to a bowl containing beaten eggs and salt. Stir well. Reheat skillet (add more oil if necessary). When oil is on the verge of smoking, pour in egg mixture. Continuously shake pan, inserting a spatula or knife around the edges to keep omelet free and to form a high, rounded edge. When the omelet is almost firm and cooked through, put a plate (upside down) over it and invert skillet, allowing omelet to drop onto plate. This is best done with a plate that fits neatly inside the skillet. Then slip the omelet back into the skillet, brown side up. Shake skillet while the second side browns. Serve at once.

Serves 2.

Spanish Omelet with Soybeans #2

1 slice bacon, cut in squares
½ tablespoon olive oil
1 slice ham, cut in squares
1 medium pork sausage, cooked and sliced
½ cup cooked soybeans, drained
Salt and freshly ground black pepper to taste
2 eggs, beaten

Fry squares of bacon in olive oil until crisp and browned. Add ham squares, slices of cooked sausage, and cooked soybeans. Add salt and freshly ground black pepper. Fry until soybeans begin to brown. Allow to cool a few minutes before adding to the bowl containing the beaten eggs. Stir well. Reheat skillet (add more oil if necessary). When oil is on the verge of smoking, pour in egg mixture. Continuously shake pan, inserting a spatula or knife around the edges to keep omelet free and to form a high, rounded edge. When the omelet is almost firm, put a plate (upside down) over it and invert skillet, allowing omelet to drop onto plate. This is best done with a plate that fits neatly inside skillet. Then slip the omelet back into skillet, brown side up. Shake skillet while the second side browns. Serve at once.

Serves 2.

Although this recipe calls for just a cup of soybeans, you will doubtless want to double or triple it after you taste these delightful snacks. A jar of roasted soybeans also makes an unusual and sure-to-please homemade gift.

Roasted Soybeans, Deep-fried

1 cup soybeans
Vegetable oil for deep-frying

Soak soybeans in water for 8 to 10 hours. Drain and spread out to dry, or pat dry with a towel. Heat oil to 350° F. Add 1 cup beans at a time and cook about 10 minutes, or until crisp. (Color should be that of roasted peanuts without skins.) Salt with plain salt, garlic salt, or other variations.

Note: There are on the market blanching baskets with holes too small for beans to fall through. (Keep in mind that beans shrink while cooking in oil.) This way all the beans can be lifted out at once.

Dry-roasted Soybeans

Soak 1 cup beans in *salted* water for 8 to 10 hours. Drain and spread out to dry. Spread in shallow pan and roast in oven at 450° F. for about 20 minutes, or until brown.

These make great snacks for everyday or for parties.

Soybean Brittle

2 cups sugar
⅓ cup water
2 tablespoons butter
Roasted soybeans

Mix 2 cups granulated sugar and about ⅓ cup water, preferably in a cast iron skillet. Cook until water evaporates and sugar begins to melt. Let it melt completely but don't allow to burn dark—it will turn amber in color. Add 2 tablespoons butter and stir until well blended. Add as many roasted soybeans as you wish. Pour at once onto an oiled cookie sheet. Spread quickly to about ¼-inch thickness— the mixture hardens quickly.

Soybean Fritters

3 eggs, beaten
¾ cup sugar
¼ teaspoon salt
1 teaspoon nutmeg
1 teaspoon cinnamon
1½ cups flour
1¾ cups soybean purée*
1½ teaspoons vanilla
1 teaspoon baking powder
    Butter or vegetable oil for frying

* *Blender method*: Purée 1-¾ cups *firmly packed* soybeans, eggs, and vanilla in the blender. Add other ingredients (flour last) and mix thoroughly. Spoon into skillet and fry on both sides until brown. (Don't fry too fast.)

Mix together eggs, sugar, salt, spices, and flour. Beat until smooth and fluffy. Add bean purée, vanilla, and baking powder. Mix thoroughly and spoon into skillet. Fry until brown on both sides. (Don't fry too fast.)
Serve hot.
Makes about 18 fritters.

"QUICKIE" RECIPES

We all have days when we are "just too busy to eat." If you have a supply of cooked soybeans in the refrigerator, you can easily come up with a tasty, high-protein dish by simply adding a cup of soybeans to almost any canned soup. Here are some good examples:

Tomato-Bean Soup

1 can condensed tomato soup
1 cup or more cooked soybeans, drained

Prepare tomato soup according to directions on the can. Add soybeans and simmer for 10 minutes. Add a pat of butter if you like.

Soy flour is also excellent for quickly enriching some soups:

Cream of Pea Soup with Soy Flour

1 can condensed cream of pea soup
¼ cup soy flour
Salt and freshly ground black pepper to taste

Prepare soup according to directions on the can. Gradually stir in soy flour and add seasonings. Simmer for a few minutes.

Cole Slaw and Bean Sprouts

To 1 container ready-made cole slaw add 1 cup finely chopped soybean sprouts. Mix well and serve.

Soybean and Spinach Omelet

1 medium onion, chopped
4 tablespoons butter
4 cups cooked soybeans, drained
  Salt and freshly ground black pepper to taste
1 package frozen chopped spinach, defrosted and
  thoroughly drained
1 tablespoon Madeira wine
6 eggs, beaten

Sauté onion in butter, add beans and spinach, and
continue cooking over low heat for 10 minutes until well
heated. Add salt and pepper and Madeira to beaten eggs,
then pour over beans and spinach. Cook a little longer until
creamy. Do not overcook. Serve immediately.

Serves 4 to 6.

Soybean Soufflé

3 cups cooked soybeans, puréed in food grinder
  or colander
4 eggs, separated
2 tablespoons minced onion
2 tablespoons chopped parsley
  Salt and freshly ground black pepper to taste
½ teaspoon thyme

Preheat oven to 325° F.

Mix egg yolks and soybean purée and *gently* heat in a
saucepan, stirring constantly, until mixture thickens
slightly. Stir in onion, parsley, salt and pepper, and thyme.

Mix well. Beat the egg whites until stiff and fold into bean mixture. Pour into well-buttered 1½-quart soufflé or baking dish, and bake for 45 minutes (or until set) in a preheated oven. Serve immediately.

Serves 6.

Cheese Soufflé

 2 tablespoons butter
 2 tablespoons flour
 1 cup milk
 ½ cup grated cheese
 ¼ cup soy granules (or soy flour)
 ¾ teaspoon salt
 4 egg yolks, beaten well
 4 egg whites, beaten until stiff

Preheat oven to 300° F.

Melt butter, blend in the flour, and gradually add milk.* Stir over low heat until sauce thickens. Add the cheese and stir until it melts and blends. Add the soy granules (or soy flour mixed with milk) and salt.

Mix egg yolks into sauce, then fold in stiffly beaten egg whites. Pour into a greased soufflé dish and bake in a preheated oven for about 1 hour, or until mixture sets. Serve immediately.

Serves 5 to 6.

* If using soy flour (instead of granules), use only ½ cup milk at this point. Mix the other ½ cup milk with soy flour.

Here is a sampling of nutritious spreads that you may not have thought of. Try them for snacks or for breakfast.

Apple Butter and Soy Flour Spread

> 3 heaping tablespoons apple butter
> 1 level tablespoon soy flour

Mix well.

Prune Butter and Soy Flour Spread

> 3 heaping tablespoons prune butter
> 1 level tablespoon soy flour

Mix well.

Sesame Tahini and Soy Flour Spread

> 1 tablespoon sesame tahini
> 1 tablespoon soy flour
> 1 tablespoon honey or molasses

Mix well. Add a little water, if necessary, to thin.

Peanut Butter and Soy Flour Spread

> 1 tablespoon peanut butter
> 1 tablespoon soy flour
> 1 tablespoon honey or molasses

Mix well. Add a little water, if necessary, to thin.

Butter, Soy Flour, and Honey Spread

2 tablespoons butter
1 tablespoon honey
2 tablespoons soy flour

Cream honey and butter. Blend in soy flour.

Two other ways of introducing protein-rich soy products into your daily menus would be to make one of the following.

TWO BASIC SAUCES

White Sauce

1 tablespoon butter
1 tablespoon flour
2 tablespoons soy flour
½ teaspoon salt
1 cup milk
Freshly ground black pepper to taste

Melt butter in a saucepan and add all dry ingredients. Stir rapidly. Slowly stir in milk and continue stirring until sauce thickens.

Makes about 1 cup.

Variation: Add ½ to 1 teaspoon sherry *or* 1 tablespoon grated cheese.

Brown Sauce

Proceed as for white sauce but substitute meat drippings for butter *and* meat broth for milk.

This simply made icing is nutritionally far superior to the usual cake icing. It just happens to be absolutely marvelous.

Creamy Cake Icing

½ cup melted butter
¼ cup honey
½ cup soy flour
½ teaspoon rum or almond flavoring (optional)

Cream butter with the honey. Gradually mix in flour. Add flavoring if desired and mix well.
Makes enough for a one-layer cake.

Soybean Cake

2 cups sugar
4 eggs, beaten
1½ cups vegetable oil
1½ cups cooked soybeans, drained
2 cups flour
1 teaspoon baking powder
1 teaspoon salt
1 teaspoon cinnamon

Mix all ingredients together. Divide mixture in half. Bake in a greased and floured pan at 350° F. for 30 minutes. If loaf pans are used, baking time is longer, according to depth of pan.

Frosting:

Cream together ¼ cup butter, 6 ounces cream cheese, 1 box confectioners' sugar, 1 teaspoon vanilla, and ½ cup chopped pecans.

Easy Soybean Spice Cake

    1 package spice cake mix
    ¼ cup vegetable oil
    3 eggs
    ½ cup milk
    1 cup cooked soybeans, drained and puréed*
    1 cup sugar
    1 teaspoon cinnamon
    ½ teaspoon allspice
    ¼ teaspoon nutmeg

Combine and beat together all ingredients until smooth. Fold in 1 cup chopped nuts (optional).
Pour into a greased 10-inch tube pan (or bundt pan). Bake in 325° F. oven for one hour and 10 minutes.

* *Blender method*: Purée soybeans and milk in blender. Mix with other ingredients and continue as above.

If you're ever in the mood for something totally different—a truly exotic dish—this spicy Nigerian pudding fills the bill nicely.

Nigerian Soybean Pudding

    1 **pound dried soybeans, soaked for 24 hours**
1½ **cups water**
    4 **tablespoons vegetable oil**
    1 **large onion, coarsely chopped**
    4 **hot chili peppers, seeded,**
                   or
      Tabasco sauce to taste
  ½ **cup minced greens (spinach, parsley, celery tops, etc.)**
  ½ **cup minced shrimp**
      Salt to taste

Purée beans in a blender in 2 batches, using the following proportions: Approximately 3 cups soaked soybeans; ¾ cup water; 2 tablespoons vegetable oil; ½ chopped onion; 2 hot peppers.

Turn both batches into a mixing bowl (mixture should have the consistency of thick pancake batter). Salt to taste and Tabasco sauce to taste (if you are using Tabasco sauce instead of hot peppers). Add minced greens and shrimp and mix thoroughly.

Turn into a 2-quart greased casserole (or mold) and cover tightly with aluminum foil. Steam for 1½ to 2 hours.

Serves 8 to 10.

Grilled Soybean Sandwich

1 cup cooked soybeans, drained
2 tablespoons catsup
  Savory salt and freshly ground black pepper to taste
  Mustard
1 tablespoon minced onion (optional)
8 slices sandwich bread
8 slices bacon, fried crisp and drained
4 slices American cheese
  Vegetable oil or melted butter

Purée soybeans with a fork or in a blender. If using blender, add catsup and 1 or 2 tablespoons water to facilitate blending. Add savory salt and pepper to taste. Add minced onion if desired.

For each sandwich spread a little mustard on a slice of bread. Spread on approximately ¼ cup of bean mixture. Put on 2 slices of crisp bacon and one slice of American cheese. Top with second slice of bread (with mustard, if you like).

Brush outside of sandwich with vegetable oil or butter. Grill on both sides until toasted.

Makes 4.

6

✖ ❋ ✖

Making Your Own
Super Protein

Tofu (or soybean curd) has been an important source of protein for centuries in other parts of the world. The Chinese call it "meat without a bone," and with good reason. For this delicately textured, cheeselike curd contains as much as 10 to 17 percent protein. Fresh tofu may look somewhat flat and tasteless. But that's more illusion than reality. When properly prepared—and the Chinese and Japanese work culinary miracles with it—it is a great delicacy. For this reason, most of the recipes in this chapter are of Oriental origin.

Most Oriental markets make tofu daily and sell it in cakes about the size and shape of a soap bar. If you are not fortunate enough to have an Oriental market in your town or neighborhood, try making tofu at home quite simply and inexpensively. One pound of dry soybeans make ¾ to 1 pound of tofu—or about 2 cups.

Use tofu in salads, omelets, soups, loaves, croquettes,

stuffings, spreads—even desserts. Scrambled tofu, properly seasoned, makes a good substitute for scrambled eggs.

The following recipe for making tofu is based on the Oriental method. It shouldn't take you more than an hour to make, and it keeps for several days.

(A list of ingredients and special seasonings used in these recipes, and their suppliers, is to be found starting on page 167. Write to them direct for supplies, or to find out the location of your nearest suppliers.)

Basic Tofu Recipe

Soak 1 pound of soybeans overnight in 2 quarts of water. The next day, drain beans (save the water for future use as stock). Pour 2 quarts of boiling water over the drained beans. Put the beans, a cup or two at a time (with some of the water), into blender, and purée. Transfer both liquid and purée to a large pot and add another 3½ quarts of boiling water. Allow to stand for 10 minutes, stirring occasionally. Have ready a colander lined with a double layer of fine cheesecloth, and through it strain the whole mixture, saving the liquid. Slowly bring liquid back to boiling point and boil for 1 minute. Cool to 185° F. and stir in 1 tablespoon of calcium sulphate* that has been mixed with ½ cup of water. Continue to stir over medium heat until mixture begins to curdle (about 2 or 3 minutes). Remove the chunks of curd as they form and place them in a colander lined with fresh cheesecloth. After removing all chunks, pour the remaining liquid through the cheesecloth-lined colander to strain out the smaller curds. Let drain completely. When cool, store the tofu in a bowl of water in the refrigerator. It

---

* Calcium sulphate (also called gypsum or plaster of Paris) comes in the form of a white powder which can be obtained in paint stores or some pharmacies.

will spoil quickly if not submerged in water. Properly stored and refrigerated it will stay fresh for days. Change water daily.

One of the easiest and nicest ways of introducing tofu into your family's diet is this omelet. It provides a great protein boost and at the same time stretches two eggs to a double serving.

Tofu Omelet

1 teaspoon vegetable oil
2 scallions, finely chopped
1 tofu cake (or 1 cup), crumbled
2 eggs, beaten
  Salt and freshly ground black pepper to taste

Lightly sauté scallions in oil. Add crumbled tofu and heat gently. Pour eggs over tofu; add salt and pepper. Cook until eggs are done to taste.

Serves 2.

In both these Japanese recipes tofu is the major ingredient. The recipes are basically identical—one being a summer dish (cold), the other a winter dish (hot). One could hardly think of a comparably simple recipe that is as tasty and nourishing.

Hiyayakko (Cold Tofu)

Tofu, well chilled, approximately 2 cakes per person, cut into 1-inch cubes, and served in individual bowls of ice water.

Sauce:
1 cup soy sauce
2 tablespoons mirin (sweet cooking sake)
3 tablespoons hanagatsuo (dried-fish shavings)
2 or 3 scallions, very thinly sliced

To remove odor from sliced scallions, put them in a strainer and hold under cold tap for a few seconds. Shake off excess water.

Put soy sauce, mirin, and hanagatsuo into a saucepan and simmer slowly for 10 minutes. Cool. Add scallions and chill. Serve the sauce in small individual bowls or in one large bowl, fondue style.

Dip the icy tofu in the sauce and enjoy! The Japanese drink beer with this dish.

Yutofu (Hot-water Tofu)

Prepare the sauce as in the above recipe, but serve the tofu cubes in hot water, and do not chill the sauce. Serve the sauce very hot (if possible, in a chafing dish). This is a perfect dish for an informal meal. Use chopsticks or fondue forks to eat with. Hot sake is the perfect accompiment.

Japanese Omelet

1 teaspoon Japanese sesame oil
1 tofu cake (or 1 cup tofu), crumbled
1 tablespoon soy sauce (or to taste)
2 eggs, beaten

Heat sesame oil; then add crumbled tofu and beat in well. Add soy sauce and continue cooking until most of soy sauce evaporates. Pour eggs over tofu and cook until eggs are done. If more salt is desired, sprinkle with soy sauce. Serves 1 or 2.

Fried Bean Curd

2 tablespoons vegetable oil
½ teaspoon dark sesame oil (optional)
½ teaspoon salt
4 cakes (about 3 cups) soybean curd, cut into small cubes
4 scallions, minced
2 tablespoons soy sauce
1 teaspoon sugar
Dash freshly ground black pepper to taste

Heat skillet over high flame; then add oil and salt. Fry bean curd until brown. Add the remaining ingredients and mix, keeping over flame. Serves 2.

Dashi is the basic broth used in almost all Japanese soups, as well as in numerous other dishes. It could not be easier to make—once the ingredients are purchased. There *are* several brands of instant dashi on the market, which come in small packages and make approximately 1 cup each. However, I prefer the following recipe.

Dashi (Japanese Soup Stock)

   6 cups water
   ½ ounce kelp* (kombu seaweed)
   ½ ounce dried bonito shavings* (hanagatsuo)

Bring the water to a boil and add the seaweed. Stir it around for 3 or 4 minutes—this releases its flavor. Remove the seaweed and add the bonito shavings. Bring to a boil again and remove from heat. The shavings will settle to the bottom of the pot in 2 or 3 minutes. Strain, and the broth is ready.

   * These two ingredients can be bought in most Oriental markets and some health food stores. They also can be ordered by mail from a good supplier (see page 169). Being dry ingredients, they are nonperishable.

Clear Soup with Tofu and Scallions

6 cups dashi or chicken stock
3 teaspoons soy sauce
 Salt to taste
 MSG to taste
1 pound (about 3 cakes) bean curd, cut into 1½-inch cubes
 or crumbled
3 or 4 scallions including tops, chopped
 Peel of 1 lemon, sliced into thin strips

Bring the stock to a boil. Add soy sauce, salt, and MSG to taste. Drop in the bean curd and simmer until it is thoroughly heated. If bean curd is cubed, remove carefully and put 2 cubes in each soup bowl. If bean curd is crumbled, use a slotted spoon to apportion bean curds into each soup bowl. Add 1 or 2 slices of lemon peel and a teaspoon or so of chopped scallions to each soup bowl. Pour boiling broth into each soup bowl. Serve immediately.
 Serves 6.

"Corn flour" soup is a rather provincial Japanese dish, but it has been very popular with Japanese students for a long time.

Kuzuhiki Soup

6 cups dashi
1 tablespoon soy sauce
 MSG to taste
 Salt to taste
1½ tablespoons corn flour
3 cakes tofu (about 1 pound), cut into 6 pieces
1 1-inch piece fresh ginger root, grated, *or* powdered ginger to taste

Bring broth to a boil and add soy sauce and MSG. Taste and add salt if necessary. Dissolve corn flour in a little water, add to soup, and cook until slightly thickened. Add tofu and simmer until heated through. Put 1 piece of tofu in each bowl, then ladle out 1 cup of broth. Sprinkle with a bit of grated ginger root or powdered ginger. Serve immediately. Serves 6.

Miso Soup with Bean Curd

6 cups dashi
MSG to taste
1 carrot, cut into thin slices
6 ounces red bean paste (aka-miso)
3 cakes tofu (about 1 pound)
2 scallions including tops, chopped

Bring the dashi to a boil, seasoning with MSG. Add carrots and cook until tender. Dissolve red bean paste in a little of the hot stock. Add to saucepan and mix together well until smooth. Add bean curd and bring to a boil. Add chopped scallions, simmer for 1 minute. Serve immediately. Serves 6.

Tofu and Soybean Sprout Omelet

2 tablespoons vegetable oil
½ teaspoon sesame oil (optional)
2 or 3 scallions, chopped
1 small green pepper, chopped
1 cup soy bean sprouts
2 tablespoons soy sauce
1 teapoon sherry
2 cakes (1½ cups) tofu, crumbled
4 eggs, beaten

Heat oil(s) in a heavy skillet over a high flame. Add the scallions and green pepper, stirring quickly for 1 or 2 minutes. Add sprouts and continue stirring for 3 to 5 minutes. Add soy sauce, sherry, and tofu. When tofu is heated, add beaten eggs, stir well, and cook until done.

Serves 2 or 3.

Eggs and Soybean Curd

    5 tablespoons light soy sauce
    3 tablespoons mirin (sweet rice wine)
    1 cup dried bonito shavings (hanagatsuo)
      About 1 pound tofu, cut in 1-inch cubes
    3 eggs, beaten
    ⅛ teaspoon MSG

Put soy sauce, mirin, and hanagatsuo in a skillet and bring to a boil. Then add the bean curd, cover, and simmer for about 5 minutes. Mix MSG with beaten eggs and pour over bean curd. Cover with lid and cook gently until eggs are done. Serve immediately.

Serves 2 or 3.

Basic Fried Tofu

    ½ cup water
      Soy sauce
    1 teaspoon cornstarch
    2 tablespoons vegetable oil
    1 teaspoon salt
    2 slices fresh ginger (or ¼ teaspoon powdered ginger)
    3 cakes tofu (about 1 pound), cut into 1-inch cubes
    2 or 3 scallions, including tops, cut into ½-inch lengths
      Steamed rice to serve

Combine the water, soy sauce, and cornstarch, set aside.

Heat oil in a skillet over a high flame. Throw in salt and ginger, then add tofu cubes. Heat 2 to 4 minutes over high flame, being careful not to break up cubes. Add the scallions. Then pour in soy-cornstarch mixture. Shake the pan (or stir gently) until the sauce thickens and covers each cube with a translucent amber glaze (about 1 or 2 minutes).

Serve with steamed rice.

Serves 3-4.

Variation: Leftover roast pork may be diced and sautéed in the pan before the tofu is added.

Chinese Tofu Soup

½ cup diced leftover pork

Marinade:
¼ teaspoon cornstarch
1 tablespoon soy sauce
½ teaspoon vegetable oil
½ teaspoon sherry

1 quart chicken stock
1 cup cabbage, chopped
2 tablespoons chopped bamboo shoots, fresh or canned
2 chopped water chestnuts, fresh or canned
2 cakes tofu, cut into 1-inch cubes
Salt and freshly ground black pepper to taste
⅛ teaspoon MSG
¼ teaspoon sugar
Few drops of Japanese sesame oil (optional)

Mix marinade and add to cut-up pork in a bowl.

Bring stock to a boil. Add pork (undrained) and continue cooking for 3 minutes. Then drop in vegetables and bean curd and cook for 3 minutes more. Add seasonings (including sesame oil) and remove from heat.

Serves 4.

This Japanese soup is light *and* filling. It'll take only a few minutes more than reaching for a can of soup on the shelf.

Japanese Curd Soup

2½ cups dashi (see recipe on page 106)
3 tablespoons miso (soybean paste)
¾ cup tofu

Combine dashi and miso and stir until paste is completely dissolved. Heat (but don't boil), then add tofu. Heat thoroughly and serve immediately.

Serves 2.

7

Soybean Sprouts

HOW TO MAKE SOYBEAN SPROUTS

Have you ever thought of gardening right in your kitchen? Now's the time to try. Sprouting is probably the simplest form of home food production on record. You don't need sophisticated equipment (although there are sprouters available in health food and specialty stores). You don't even have to worry about the weather outside. It all happens right on the kitchen shelf.

There are several methods for sprouting the beans, but the simplest is the following:

Take 1 cup of dried soybeans, sort them, and wash them thoroughly. Soak overnight in 4 cups of lukewarm water. The following morning drain the beans (save water for cooking) and put them into a large flower pot or colander. Remember the beans will expand to 6 times their original bulk. If a flower pot is used, place wire mesh or cloth over the hole in the bottom. Cover container with a damp cloth and put in a dark, warm place. Inside the broom closet perhaps; or on a top kitchen shelf (the best temperature is about 75° F.). Flood with lukewarm water 4 or 5 times a day during the sprouting period, draining the water out each time. In 4 to 6 days the sprouts will be 2 or 3 inches long and ready to eat. (In the summer sprouts will be ready in about 2 or 3 days.) The important thing is to keep the beans wet at all times—don't let them dry out! However, they must have good drainage; otherwise, they will develop a mold.

Store sprouts in the refrigerator in a plastic bag. They should be used immediately but will stay fresh for 2 or 3 days.

Sprouts can be cooked and served as a plain vegetable. Cook only long enough to remove the raw taste. Do not overcook.

FOUR BASIC COOKING METHODS

Blanch: Put sprouts in blanching basket (or deep-fry basket) and immerse in boiling water for about 3 minutes.

Sauté: Heat a small amount of oil in a skillet. Add sprouts and a teaspoon of water. Cover and cook about 5 minutes.

Steam: Put sprouts in steamer and steam about 5 minutes.

Stir-fry: (*Chow*—the Chinese method) Heat small amount of vegetable oil in a heavy skillet over high flame. Add sprouts and stir constantly to avoid burning (they should be done in about 3 to 5 minutes). The object of stir-frying is to "cook out" the raw flavor of the ingredients without destroying the color, flavor, texture, and nutrients.

After cooking, serve like any other simple vegetable —with butter, salt and pepper, or sesame oil and soy sauce, etc.

Soybean Sprout Salad

Sauce:

¼ cup wine vinegar
2 tablespoons soy sauce
1 tablespoon vegetable oil
1 teaspoon dark sesame oil
½ teaspoon sugar
½ teaspoon Tabasco sauce
⅛ teaspoon MSG

2 teaspoons vegetable oil
1 egg, beaten
1 pound fresh soybean sprouts (about 6 cups)
6 scallions, including tops, finely sliced

Prepare sauce by mixing together all ingredients, stirring well, and chill. Heat 2 teaspoons oil in a small skillet. Then cook egg so that it forms a flat, dry pancake. Remove to a plate, cool, and cut into thin strips about 2 inches long.

Wash bean sprouts thoroughly and steam or blanch for 3 to 5 minutes. Drain and splash with cold water to stop cooking process. Mix egg, scallions, and sprouts. Chill. Stir sauce and pour over sprout mixture just before serving.

Serves 4.

Hot Soybean Sprout Salad

    1 stalk celery, sliced thin
    1 small onion, sliced
    1 small green pepper, cut into thin strips
    2 tablespoons vegetable oil
    ½ clove garlic, minced (optional)
    2 cups soybean sprouts
    1 tablespoon soy sauce
      Salt and freshly ground black pepper to taste

Gently sauté celery, onion, green pepper (and garlic) in oil. Add sprouts and soy sauce. Cover and cook gently for about 8 minutes. Salt and pepper to taste. Serve hot, or allow to cool to room temperature.

Serves 2.

Soybean Sprouts and Bacon Casserole

    ¾ cup stock
    1 tablespoon soy sauce
    1 teaspoon sugar
    ⅛ teaspoon MSG
    2 teaspoons cornstarch
    ½ teaspoon salt
    4 slices bacon, cut into small pieces
    2 tablespoons vegetable oil
    2 slices onion
    3 cups sprouts

Combine stock, soy sauce, sugar, MSG, cornstarch, and salt in a bowl. Set aside. Fry bacon pieces until they are brown and crisp. Drain and set aside.

Heat oil in a 10-inch skillet. Fry onion slices until soft

and translucent. Remove from skillet and set aside with bacon.

Now add sprouts to skillet (be sure they are well drained to minimize splattering) and stir-fry, turning constantly to prevent burning. Do not overcook! Add stock mixture, bacon and onion slices to sprouts and stir until mixture thickens. Serve immediately.

Serves 3.

Soybean Sprouts and Bacon

¼ pound bacon
2 cups blanched or steamed soybean sprouts
1 teaspoon soy sauce (or to taste)

Cut bacon into strips and fry until crisp. Add sprouts and soy sauce. Toss lightly and cook for about 3 minutes. Serves 2.

Stir-fried Soybean Sprouts and Peppers

2 tablespoons vegetable oil
1 teaspoon salt
Thin slice ginger (or ⅛ teaspoon powdered ginger)
3 or 4 green peppers, washed, seeded, and thinly sliced
2 hot chilis, seeded and minced
¾ pound soybean sprouts (4 to 5 cups)
¼ cup chicken stock (or water)
1 teaspoon sherry
¼ teaspoon MSG
¼ teaspoon sugar

Heat skillet over high flame. Combine oil, salt, and ginger in a skillet. Then add peppers and chilis and stir for 1 minute. Add bean sprouts and mix well. Pour in stock, cover, and continue cooking for 3 minutes more. Add sherry, MSG, and sugar to the mixture; mix well.

Serves 3 or 4.

Soy Sprout Soup

1½ quarts chicken or beef stock
 2 cups bean sprouts
 3 eggs, beaten
 3 tablespoons chives or scallions, minced
    Salt and freshly ground black pepper to taste

Heat stock; add whole bean sprouts. Simmer for 3 to 5 minutes. Remove from heat and stir in the beaten eggs. Season with salt and pepper. Garnish with chives or scallions.

Serves 4 to 6.

Soybean Sprout Soup with Beef

 3 chopped green onions (reserve tops)
 1 clove garlic, minced
 ¼ pound lean beef, cut into small, thin slices
 4 tablespoons soy sauce
 ½ teaspoon Japanese sesame oil
 3 cups soybean sprouts
 2 quarts water
    Salt and freshly ground black pepper to taste

Put onions, garlic, meat, sesame oil, and half of soy sauce into a soup pot. Mix and cook until the meat is well seared—about 15 minutes. Add the bean sprouts, mix together, and cook for about 3 minutes. Add 2 quarts of water and the rest of the soy sauce. Cook for 30 minutes, or until the sprouts and meat are tender. Salt and pepper to taste. Add finely chopped onion tops and serve.

Serves 8.

There are many variations on this ancient Spanish dish. It is a soup for the hot summer months when fresh vegetables are plentiful. Soy sprouts blend in beautifully for an especially nourishing variation.

Gazpacho

2 ripe tomatoes, coarsely chopped
1 small green pepper, seeded and chopped
½ cucumber, sliced
1 clove garlic, chopped
1 small onion, quartered
2 tablespoons olive oil
2 tablespoons wine vinegar
¼ teaspoon cumin powder
Salt to taste
2 cups ice water
2 cups soybean sprouts

Put all ingredients except sprouts in a blender. Blend on medium speed for only a few seconds. Add sprouts to mixture, and blend again, taking care that sprouts do not completely dissolve.

Serves 4 or 5.

Now for some recipes from the Orient, where they know how to use bean sprouts in so many delicious ways.

Vegetable Chop Suey

½ cup vegetable oil
2 large green peppers, coarsely chopped or cut into strips
1 cup onion, thinly sliced
2 cups celery, cut medium-coarse
3 cups bean sprouts
1 cup boiling water
1 tablespoon cornstarch
1 tablespoon sherry
2 tablespoons soy sauce
⅛ teaspoon MSG
Salt and freshly ground black pepper to taste
Hot noodles or rice to serve

Heat oil in a large skillet. Add peppers, onion, celery, and sprouts. Sauté for 3 to 5 minutes, but do not brown. Add boiling water. Cover and simmer for about another 7 minutes. Mix cornstarch with soy sauce and sherry, and add to vegetables. Cook slowly until mixture thickens (about 5 minutes). Add MSG and salt and pepper to taste. Serve with noodles or rice.
Serves 4 to 6.

Sauteed Soybean Sprouts

3 tablespoons vegetable oil
½ teaspoon Japanese sesame oil
2 or 3 scallions, finely chopped
4 cups soybean sprouts
2 or 3 tablespoons soy sauce
½ cup sliced water chestnuts
½ cup sliced mushrooms

Heat oils in a heavy skillet. Add scallions and cook for 1 minute. Then add the sprouts and fry, stirring constantly, for 1 minute more.

Add soy sauce, water chestnuts, and mushrooms to the beans. Cook, stirring, for 4 or 5 minutes. Serve immediately. Serves 4 to 6.

Egg Foo Yung

3 medium dried mushrooms
5 tablespoons vegetable oil
1 small onion, finely minced
4 scallions, thinly sliced
3 cups fresh soybean sprouts
¾ cup cooked meat (pork, shrimp, or chicken), cut into shreds
2 tablespoons soy sauce
1½ teaspoons salt
1 teaspoon sugar
6 eggs, beaten

Soak mushrooms in warm water to cover for 30 minutes. Drain and rinse. Cut into thin strips.

Heat 1 tablespoon oil in a skillet. Briefly sauté onion, scallions, and mushrooms. Add sprouts, then the meat. Mix together well. Add the soy sauce, salt, and sugar, and combine with the vegetables in the skillet over high heat. Remove from skillet and set aside to cool. When cool, combine with beaten eggs.

Heat 2 teaspoons oil in a small skillet (preferably cast iron) over a low flame. Pour in sufficient amount of mixture to cover bottom of skillet. Brown one side and turn carefully to retain pancake shape. When done, place on a platter in a warm oven. Apportion egg mixture so as to make 6 pancakes.

Once these have been cooked, they can be reheated in a double boiler or steamer.

Sauce:

¾ cup chicken stock
1 tablespoon soy sauce
½ teaspoon salt
⅛ teaspoon MSG
1 tablespoon cornstarch

Bring chicken stock to a boil in a small saucepan. Add soy sauce, salt, and MSG. Mix the cornstarch with 1½ tablespoons water and add to sauce, stirring until mixture thickens. Pour over egg pancakes and serve immediately.

Chow Mein

2 cups soybean sprouts
2 cups onion, thinly sliced
4 tablespoons oil
2 cups cooked meat (beef, pork, or chicken), diced or cut into strips
1 small can (6 ounces) mushrooms, sliced, with liquid
3 tablespoons soy sauce
 Salt and freshly ground black pepper to taste
2 tablespoons cornstarch
1 tablespoon sherry
⅛ teaspoon MSG
 Hot noodles or rice to serve

Cook sprouts in 2 cups boiling water for 5 minutes and drain. Reserve water. In a large skillet sauté onion in oil until golden brown. Add cooked sprouts, meat, sliced mushrooms with liquid, and soy sauce. Add enough water (from sprouts) to cover. Salt and pepper to taste. Thicken with cornstarch, add sherry and MSG, cover, and cook for 10 minutes. Serve with noodles or rice.

Serves 6.

Scrambled Eggs with Soybean Sprouts

2 or 3 scallions, finely chopped
½ teaspoon salt
   Freshly ground black pepper to taste
4 eggs, slightly beaten
2 cups soybean sprouts, blanched or steamed
1 tablespoon butter

Combine scallions, and salt and pepper with beaten eggs. Let stand for 5 or 10 minutes. Heat butter and sprouts in a skillet. Add egg mixture to sprouts and stir. Cook until done.

Serves 2.

Soybean Sprout Omelet

4 eggs, beaten
2 tablespoons milk
   Salt and freshly ground black pepper to taste
1½ tablespoons butter
1 cup soybean sprouts
1 small scallion, minced

Combine eggs, milk, and salt and pepper. Heat the butter in an omelet pan. Pour in egg mixture and cook until omelet begins to set. Sprinkle in sprouts and minced scallion. Fold over and slip into a warm dish.

Serves 1 or 2.

Soybean Sprouts au Gratin

1 pound soybean sprouts (about 6 cups)
3 tablespoons butter
2 tablespoons flour
1 cup cream (or milk)
1 cup grated Swiss cheese
  Salt and freshly ground black pepper to taste
  Paprika to taste
¼ cup Italian flavored bread crumbs

Steam or blanch sprouts for 3 to 5 minutes. Heat butter and stir in flour; then add cream (or milk). Add ½ cup grated cheese and the seasonings; stir until cheese melts. Add sprouts. Pour the mixture into a greased casserole. Sprinkle with bread crumbs and remaining cheese. Bake at 350° F. until crust browns.
    Serves 4.

This recipe, as well as the following ones incorporating just vegetables, has a crisp chewiness that is very satisfying. You feel you *are* getting real nourishment!

Cabbage and Soybean Sprouts

3 tablespoons vegetable oil
½ teaspoon Japanese sesame oil
2 or 3 tablespoons soy sauce
4 cups shredded cabbage
1 tablespoon vinegar
2 cups soybean sprouts
  Salt and freshly ground black pepper to taste

Heat oils in a heavy skillet or a casserole with a lid. Add the soy sauce and cabbage. Cover and cook until translucent (5 to 10 minutes). Now add vinegar and sprouts, stir, and cook about 5 minutes longer, until sprouts are tender. Salt and pepper to taste.

Serves 6.

Fried Celery and Soybean Sprouts

> 2 tablespoons vegetable oil
> ½ teaspoon Japanese sesame oil
> 2 cups celery, cut into 1-inch pieces
> 2 cups soybean sprouts
> 1 teaspoon salt
> Freshly ground black pepper to taste

Heat oils in a heavy skillet. Sauté the celery for 2 to 5 minutes. Add the bean sprouts, seasoning with salt and pepper. Cook for 5 minutes more.

Serves 4.

Peking Soybean Sprouts

> 2 tablespoons vegetable oil
> 2 cups soybean sprouts
> 2 teaspoons sliced ginger root (or ½ teaspoon powdered ginger)
> ½ teaspoon salt
> 3 scallions, including tops, chopped
> 2 tablespoons soy sauce

Heat oil in a heavy skillet. Sauté the sprouts for 3 to 5 minutes, stirring constantly. Add ginger and salt. Cover and continue cooking for 3 minutes more. Stir in scallions and soy sauce. Cook for 2 minutes.

Serve 3 to 4.

Soybean Sprouts and Sauteed Vegetables

1 small onion, sliced
1 stalk celery, sliced thin
½ green pepper, cut into strips
2 tablespoons vegetable oil
½ teaspoon Japanese sesame oil (optional)
1 pound soybean sprouts (about 6 cups)
2 tablespoons soy sauce
Salt and freshly ground black pepper to taste

Sauté onion, celery, and green pepper in oil(s) for about 3 to 5 minutes. Add the sprouts and soy sauce. Cover and cook gently for 5 to 8 minutes. Season with salt and pepper.

Serves 8.

A great new variation on an old favorite. Make these for your next picnic or buffet and watch them disappear.

Eggs Stuffed with Soybean Sprouts

6 hard-boiled eggs
1 cup soybean sprouts
1 tablespoon soy sauce
1 teaspoon vegetable oil
½ teaspoon Tabasco sauce
½ teaspoon curry powder
1 teaspoon chives, minced
Salt and freshly ground black pepper to taste
Paprika

Cut eggs in half lengthwise and take out yolks. Chop soybean sprouts very fine and mash together with the egg yolks. Add soy sauce, oil, Tabasco sauce, curry powder, chives, and salt and pepper. Mix well and fill each egg half. Sprinkle with paprika and serve.

Makes 12.

Hamburger patties never tasted so succulent.

Hamburger and Soybean Sprout Patties

1 pound lean ground beef
2 scallions, including tops, minced
2 cups soybean sprouts, minced
2 tablespoons soy sauce
   Salt and freshly ground black pepper to taste
   Flour

Mix all ingredients (except flour) well. Shape into 4 patties. Dip each patty into flour and sauté on both sides until done.

Serves 4.

Soybean Sprout and Tuna Fish Sandwich Spread

1 7-ounce can tuna, flaked
3 scallions, minced
1 small green pepper, finely chopped
1 cup soybean sprouts, finely chopped
¾ cup mayonnaise
1 teaspoon soy sauce
    Salt and freshly ground black pepper to taste
8 slices sandwich bread

Mix all ingredients well. Spread on bread.
Makes 4 sandwiches.

This has proved an excellent (and practical) dish for post-Thanksgiving. And a most welcome change from the usual leftover-turkey dishes.

Soybean Sprouts and Leftover Turkey

    2 tablespoons soy sauce
    1 teaspoon Tabasco sauce
    1 teaspoon vinegar
    2 tablespoons vegetable oil
      Salt and freshly ground black pepper to taste
    2 cups soybean sprouts, steamed or blanched
    1 cup chopped celery
    3 scallions, chopped fine
    2 cups turkey meat, chopped

Mix together well the soy sauce, Tabasco, vinegar, vegetable oil, and seasonings. Combine bean sprouts, celery, and scallions with turkey; then pour sauce over mixture. Toss and serve.

Serves 4.

8

❧ ✤ ❧

Mostly Desserts

Now we come to soy flour, which has some unusual qualities. Apart from its unequaled nutritional benefits, it has some characteristics that make it most valuable in home baking. Soy flour makes dough more pliable, less sticky, and easier to handle, as well as enriching the crust color, enhancing flavor, and retarding fat absorption. (This last is most welcome in cooking doughnuts or croquettes.) Cakes and breads containing soy flour have an unusual tenderness and fine texture. Crusts are thin and crisp and appetizingly amber-toned in color. Cookies, waffles, and pancakes brown evenly and do not stick. Doughnuts and croquettes are golden brown, light, and tender inside, and never turn out greasy.

Soy flour can be substituted for up to as much as 50 percent of wheat flour in some recipes. Some cookies and muffins are perfectly delicious made entirely with soy flour, but in general the results are tastier and lighter when only part soy is used—say 20 to 30 percent. A good rule of thumb: less soy flour makes a lighter product, more soy flour makes a heavier product. Of course, the less soy flour used means less protein gained. Regardless of what percentage is used, however, one has the satisfaction of knowing that incalculable nutritional riches are being added to any recipe.

Homemade White Bread

1 cup milk
½ cup shortening
1 .2-ounce yeast cake in ½ cup warm water
2 tablespoons sugar
1 teaspoon salt
3 eggs, beaten
3 cups all-purpose flour
1 cup soy flour

Heat milk, shortening, sugar, and salt until shortening is melted. Cool to lukewarm and add dissolved yeast cake. Then add eggs and flour in alternating batches. Beat well until smooth, and put in a greased bowl. Cover with a clean dishtowel and put in a warm place (about 80° F.); allow to rise (about 30 minutes). Push down, divide into 2 equal parts and put in 2 greased loaf pans (8½-by-4½ inches). Leave to rise again (about 30 minutes) and bake at 350° F. until done (about 30 minutes). Brush tops with butter while hot if you don't want a crust.

Kneaded Soy-Wheat Bread

2 .2-ounce cakes yeast
3 cups milk, scalded and cooled to lukewarm
1 tablespoon honey
1½ tablespoons salt
2 tablespoons dark molasses
5½ cups whole wheat flour
1 cup soy flour, sifted

Dissolve yeast in 1 cup milk and honey. Let stand for 10 minutes. Add rest of milk, salt, and molasses. Mix well. Stir in half the flours and heat until smooth. Slowly add and beat in remaining flour. Cover with clean towel. Set in a warm place (about 80° F.) out of drafts for 1½ hours, and let rise. Turn onto a floured board and knead for 5 minutes, adding only enough flour to handle dough. (To knead, fold dough toward you and then push away with heels of hands in a rocking motion; rotate dough a quarter turn. Repeat until dough is smooth.)

Roll dough into a rectangle, approximately 18-by-9 inches. Cut into 2 9-inch squares. Roll each one up, press ends to seal; fold ends under. Place seam-side down in greased loaf pans (8½-by-4½ inches).

Let rise again in a warm place for 30 minutes. Bake at 375° F. for about 40 minutes.

Turn out onto wire racks to cool. To store, wrap in wax paper and put in bread box or some other tightly covered container.

Simple Soy-Wheat Bread

3 cups wholewheat flour, unsifted
1 cup soy flour, sifted
1 teaspoon salt
1 .2-ounce cake yeast
1½ cups lukewarm water
1 teaspoon dark molasses

Put whole wheat flour in a bowl and sift in soy flour. Add salt and mix well. Dissolve yeast in ⅓ cup lukewarm water and let stand for 10 minutes. Mix with the remaining water and molasses. Pour in flour mixture. Mix well by hand until mixture becomes elastic and leaves sides of bowl clean. Place in a warmed and oiled loaf pan (8½-by-4½ inches). Cover with a clean towel and put in a warm place (about 80° F.) out of drafts to rise (about 1 hour). Bake in a hot oven (450° F.) for 35 to 40 minutes.

Turn out onto wire racks and let cool. To store, wrap in wax paper and put in bread box or other tightly covered container.

The following three recipes are for breads with a difference —they all have that nutty flavor that makes them as good as cake. Or slice them thinly and serve with butter!

Tasty Soy-Nut Bread

1 cup all-purpose flour
1 cup soy flour
1 teaspoon salt
2 teaspoons baking powder
⅔ cup sugar
1 tablespoon butter
1 egg, beaten
1 cup milk
1 cup walnuts, finely chopped

Sift flours, salt, and baking powder together. In another bowl cream sugar and butter together. Add egg and mix well. Gradually add flour mixture (in fourths), alternating with milk (in thirds), beginning and ending with flour mixture. Beat until quite smooth. Stir in nuts and pour mixture into a lightly greased 1½-quart loaf pan. Let stand for 30 minutes. Meanwhile preheat oven to 350° F.

Bake for 1 hour, or until done (crisp on top). Remove from oven. Let cool for 10 minutes before removing from pan.

Mexican Fiesta Bread

½ cup hot milk
¼ cup shortening (or vegetable oil)
¼ cup sugar
1 teaspoon salt
2 .6-ounce cakes yeast
½ cup water
1 egg, beaten
½ cup mixed candied fruit and peels, finely chopped
¼ cup walnuts, chopped
¾ teaspoon cinnamon
¾ cup soy flour, sifted
2¼ cups all-purpose flour, sifted

Mix together milk, shortening, sugar, and salt. Soften yeast in water. When milk mixture is cool, stir in yeast, egg, candied fruit, nuts, and cinnamon. Add sifted flours mixing to a moderately stiff dough. Shape into a loaf and place in a greased bread pan (9¼-by-4¼ inches). Cover and let rise in a warm place (about 80° F.) until doubled in bulk—about 1 to 1½ hours. Bake in 350° to 375° F. oven for 35 to 40 minutes. Cool thoroughly before storing or slicing.

The loaf may be glazed while still warm with powdered sugar mixed to spreading consistency with water, fruit juice, or sherry.

Spicy Soy Bread

1 cup cooked soybeans, drained
½ cup milk
1 cup sugar
1 egg
1½ cups all-purpose flour
1¼ teaspoons baking powder
1 teaspoon salt
1 teaspoon cinnamon
½ teaspoon nutmeg
2 tablespoons soft butter
1 cup pecans, chopped

Preheat oven to 350° F.

Purée beans in a food grinder, colander, or blender.*
Combine with sugar, egg, and milk.

Now add all dry ingredients (sifted) to the bean-egg
mixture, then the butter. Beat until well blended. Stir in
chopped pecans. Pour into a well-greased loaf pan and bake
in a preheated oven for 1 hour, or until done.

* If using a blender, combine eggs and milk with beans before
blending. Add sugar and continue as above.

A real cake now, and it's so light and tender. Try it for a treat.

Basic Plain Cake Recipe

1 cup soy flour, sifted
1 cup all-purpose flour, sifted
3 tablespoons baking powder
¼ teaspoon salt
½ cup shortening
1 cup sugar
2 eggs, well beaten
¾ cup milk
1 teaspoon vanilla

Mix flours, baking powder, and salt. In a separate bowl, cream sugar and shortening until light and fluffy. Add eggs and mix well, then add dry ingredients and milk—alternating batches of each. Stir well after each addition. Add vanilla. Bake in 2 greased 8-inch cake pans in a 375° F. oven for 30 minutes. Cool and spread with your favorite frosting.

Honey Cake

½ cup vegetable oil
2 eggs, beaten
1 cup honey
1 cup strong black coffee (make with 2 heaping teaspoons
   instant espresso)
¾ cup sugar
2 teaspoons baking powder
1 teaspoon cinnamon
1 teaspoon allspice
2 cups all-purpose flour
1 cup soy flour
½ cup chopped almonds (or other nuts)

Mix oil and eggs, and add honey and coffee. Mix together until blended. Add sugar gradually and mix well. Now add all dry ingredients (sifted together). Add nuts and mix very well.

Pour into a greased loaf pan (9-by-5 inches) and bake at 325° F. for about 1 hour and 10 minutes.

For a delicious, moist dessert, serve this warm, straight from the oven. Or chilled, it still tastes just as good.

Banana-Nut Loaf

1 cup sugar
½ cup butter
2 bananas, mashed fine
2 eggs, beaten
1 cup walnuts, chopped
2 cups soy flour
1 teaspoon salt

Mix sugar and butter; add the mashed bananas. Now add eggs, flour, nuts, and salt, and mix together well. Bake slowly in a buttered loaf pan in a 300° to 325° oven for about 1 hour and 15 minutes.

Note: If using a blender, mix banana chunks with eggs at slow speed. Add to sugar and butter, and follow rest of instructions.

Mazapan Loaf

½ pound butter
1½ cups sugar
6 eggs
2 cups soy flour, sifted
1 teaspoon vanilla

Cream butter and sugar until light. Add unbeaten eggs, one at a time, thoroughly mixing each egg into the batter. Add flour and beat until smooth and very light. Add vanilla. Bake at 250° F. for 30 minutes. Increase heat 25° every 30 minutes until done. It should take a total of 2 hours, by which time your oven will be at 325° F.

Prune Loaf

½ cup shortening
1 cup sugar
2 eggs, separated
¾ cup milk
1½ cups soy flour
⅔ cup stewed prunes, seeded and mashed
½ teaspoon each salt, cinnamon, nutmeg, and allspice
1 teaspoon baking powder

Preheat oven to 300° F.

Blend together shortening and sugar; then add egg yolks (reserving whites). Add milk and flour. Add prunes, spices, and baking powder. In a separate bowl beat egg whites until they form peaks. Fold into batter. Pour into a greased loaf pan and bake in a 300° F. oven for 1 hour.

Spice Cake

    1 cup sugar
    ¼ cup butter
    1 cup milk
    ½ cup chopped pecans (or walnuts)
    ½ cup seedless raisins
    1 cup all-purpose flour
    ½ cup soy flour
    1½ teaspoons baking powder
    1 teaspoon cinnamon
    ¼ teaspoon nutmeg
    ½ teaspoon cloves
    1 rounded teaspoon cocoa powder
    ½ teaspoon salt
    ½ teaspoon vanilla

Cream sugar and butter; then add milk, raisins, and nuts. Sift together flours, baking powder, spices, cocoa, and salt. Gradually add to liquid mixture and mix well until smooth. Add vanilla. Mix again. Pour into a lightly greased 8-by-8-inch pan and bake at 350° F. for about 40 minutes.

This is an excellent and unusual (but perfectly easy) cake to serve for your friends who love crisp flavors.

Burmese Cake

½ cup soy flour
¾ cup farina
1 teaspoon baking powder
½ cup butter
1 cup sugar
4 eggs, separated
1½ cups coconut, finely chopped
1 teaspoon vanilla

Preheat oven to 350° F.
Sift flour, farina, and baking powder together. Separately cream butter and sugar until fluffy. Beat in egg yolks, one yolk at a time. Blend well. Now add flour mixture, coconut, and vanilla and mix together well. Fold in stiffly beaten egg whites. Pour into 2 buttered 8-inch cake pans. Bake in a preheated oven for about 20 minutes, or until done.

Cool on cake rack. Spread with your favorite icing, or serve with whipped cream and more coconut.

Quick and Easy Cheese Bundt Loaf

1 .2-ounce cake yeast
½ cup lukewarm water
½ cup milk
¼ cup butter
1¾ cups all-purpose flour
½ cup soy flour
2 tablespoons sugar
1 rounded teaspoon salt
1 egg

Filling:

Combine ¼ cup warm butter, ½ teaspoon Italian herb seasoning (or pinch of mixed herbs), and ½ clove garlic minced. Add 1 cup grated Swiss cheese. Mix well.

Dissolve yeast in water and set aside. In a saucepan heat milk and butter until warm.

In a large mixing bowl, combine 1 cup all-purpose flour with soy flour, sugar, salt, warm-milk mixture, dissolved yeast, and egg. Blend together with rotary or electric beater (medium speed) until smooth (2 or 3 minutes); or beat by hand. Gradually stir in remaining ¾ cup all-purpose flour. Spoon and spread ½ the batter into a well-greased loaf pan (9-by-5-inches). Spread with filling. Top with remaining batter. If filling is not entirely covered, batter will cover it during rising. Cover with clean towel and let rise in a warm place (80° F.) out of drafts until it doubles (about 1 hour). Bake at 350° F. for 35 to 40 minutes until golden brown. Invert immediately. Remove from pan. It's best served still warm.

Fluffy Waffles

    1 cup all-purpose flour
    1 cup soy flour
    2 teaspoons baking powder
    1 teaspoon sugar
    1 teaspoon salt
    2 eggs, separated
 1⅔ cups milk
    6 tablespoons melted butter

Sift together flours, baking powder, sugar, and salt. Add beaten egg yolks and milk and butter. Beat until smooth.

Fold in stiffly beaten egg whites. Bake on a hot waffle iron until crisp and brown.

Makes 10 to 12 waffles.

Hearty All-Soy Pancakes

2 cups milk
4 eggs, separated
1 teaspoon salt
Approximately 1½ cups soy flour, sifted

Put egg yolks, milk, and salt in a mixing bowl and beat well. Stir in flour. Fold in stiffly beaten egg whites, mixing thoroughly. Spoon onto a hot oiled griddle or oiled skillet. Brown lightly on both sides.

Serves 4 to 6.

Pancakes

1 cup all-purpose flour
1 cup soy flour
3 teaspoons baking powder
½ rounded teaspoon salt
2 eggs, well beaten
1¾ cups milk
4 tablespoons melted shortening

Sift together flours, baking powder, and salt. Pour in beaten eggs, milk, and shortening. Mix together well. Drop batter by spoonfuls onto a lightly greased hot griddle or heavy skillet. When bubbles appear, turn cakes and brown on other side. Do not turn again.

Makes 15 to 18 pancakes.

These light, buttery crêpes are perfect for a quick and simple dessert. They also add a delightful touch to special breakfasts and brunches.

French Pancakes

2 eggs
2 heaping tablespoons soy flour
3 tablespoons milk
½ teaspoon sugar
   Dash of nutmeg

Combine all ingredients and beat until well blended. Heat a small skillet and brush with melted butter. Pour in a small amount of batter (about 1 tablespoon). Quickly rotate skillet to spread batter. Cook for approximately 1 minute; flip over and cook for approximately 1 minute on the other side. Brush skillet with more butter and continue. Serve with additional butter and jam, jelly, or honey.

Makes 7 or 8 pancakes.

Basic Muffin Recipe

Follow the Basic Plain Cake Recipe (page 136). Divide mix into 2 greased muffin pans and bake at 375° F. for 25 to 30 minutes.

Raisin-Nut Muffins

1½ cups soy flour
2 teaspoons baking powder
½ teaspoon salt
2 eggs, separated
¼ cup sugar
1 cup milk
1 tablespoon vegetable oil
1 teaspoon vanilla flavoring
¼ cup raisins
¼ cup walnuts, chopped

Preheat oven to 375° F.
Sift together flour, baking powder, and salt. Beat the egg yolks until light; mix well with sugar, and add milk and oil. Mix and beat well. Pour the egg mixture into dry ingredients and blend well. Add raisins and walnuts; mix thoroughly. Fold in stiffly beaten egg whites and vanilla flavoring. Spoon into muffin tin and bake for about 30 minutes.
Makes 8 muffins.

Mother's Biscuits

1 cup soy flour
1 cup all-purpose flour
4 teaspoons baking powder
1 teaspoon salt
½ cup shortening
⅔ cup milk

Preheat oven to 425° F.
Sift together all the dry ingredients. Cut in shortening

and add milk. Mix until dough sticks together. Roll to ⅓ to ½-inch thickness on a floured dough board. Cut out and bake on an ungreased cookie sheet in a preheated oven for 12 to 15 minutes.

Makes about 18.

Buttermilk Biscuits

¾ cup soy flour
¾ cup all-purpose flour
1 teaspoon salt
1 teaspoon baking powder
¼ teaspoon baking soda
⅓ cup shortening
½ cup buttermilk

Sift together dry ingredients. Cut in shortening, then add buttermilk. Mix well and roll to ½-inch thickness on a floured dough board. Cut out and place close together on a greased cookie sheet. Bake in 425° F. oven for about 12 minutes.

Makes about 1 dozen.

Finger Rolls

1 cup warm water
1 .2-ounce cake yeast
3 eggs, beaten
1 large teaspoon salt
½ cup sugar
½ cup melted butter
1 cup soy flour
3½ cups all-purpose flour

Dissolve yeast in the water. Then mix first 4 ingredients. Add the sifted flours, and mix well. Let rise for 4 hours and put in a well-covered bowl in the refrigerator overnight. Take a third of the dough and roll into pie shape. Cut into 12 wedge-shaped pieces and roll up, starting with the base of the triangle. Brush with melted butter and let rise in a warm place for 3 to 4 hours. Bake for 7 to 12 minutes in a 425° F. oven. These keep very well if refrigerated. Makes about 3 dozen.

Old-fashioned Doughnuts

```
3 cups all-purpose flour
1 cup soy flour
1 .6 ounces cake yeast
1 cup warm water
⅝ cup scalded milk, cooled to lukewarm
¼ cup vegetable oil
½ cup sugar or honey
½ teaspoon salt
1 egg, beaten
  Cooking fat for deep-frying
  Confectioners' sugar
```

Sift flours together. Dissolve yeast in water. Add milk. Add ½ of flour and mix well. Cover and let stand in a warm place for about 3 hours. Cream the remaining ingredients (except for the flour). Incorporate flour batter as well as the remaining flour. Mix well and beat smooth. Turn out onto a lightly floured dough board and knead lightly. Cover and allow to rise overnight.

Next morning knead again and let rise until doubled in bulk. Roll out, cut out with doughnut cutters, and fry in deep fat at 325° F. until brown. Turn only once. Drain on absorbent towels. Shake in paper sack with powdered sugar. Makes about 2 dozen.

Crullers

 3 cups all-purpose flour
1¼ cups soy flour
 3 tablespoons baking powder
 ¾ teaspoon salt
 ¾ teaspoon nutmeg
 3 tablespoons melted butter
 1 cup sugar
 3 eggs, beaten
 1 cup and 1 tablespoon milk
   Cooking fat for deep-frying
   Confectioners' sugar

Sift together dry ingredients (except sugar) and blend well. Cream butter and sugar together. Add the eggs and mix well. Then add milk and mix well. Add dry ingredients and mix thoroughly.

Roll out onto a well-floured dough board. Cut into strips about 1 inch wide and 5 inches long. Twist 2 or 3 times, and press ends firmly together, making a ring.

Drop into deep fat (345° F.). Fry until golden brown (turn only once). Drain on absorbent towels and dip into or dust with powdered sugar.

Makes about 20.

Children (and, we're told, grown-ups too) love these crunchy cookies. These, packed in a lunch box, can only be good for you!

Nut Wafers

1 cup light brown sugar
1 egg
Pinch of salt
1 cup almonds, chopped very finely, or "grated" in a blender
½ cup soy flour

Mix all ingredients in the order given. Drop from a teaspoon onto a buttered cookie sheet. Leave plenty of room to spread. Bake at 375° F. for 25 to 30 minutes. Watch! Makes 12.

Note: Pecans or walnuts may be used instead of almonds.

Cinnamon-Nut Cookies

½ cup light brown sugar
½ cup honey
1 egg
3 ounces walnuts (about 1 cup)
¼ teaspoon salt
½ teaspoon cinnamon
1 cup soy flour

Mix ingredients in the order given. Drop from a teaspoon onto a buttered cookie sheet. Leave plenty of room to spread. Bake at 350° to 375° F. for about 12 minutes. Makes 12 to 15.

Peanut Butter Cookies

1 cup butter
2 cups sugar
1 cup peanut butter
2 eggs
3 cups soy flour

Cream butter, then mix in sugar. Blend in remaining ingredients.

Shape into 2 long rolls (1½ to 2 inches in diameter). Slice; bake on a greased cookie sheet in a 375° F. oven for 10 to 15 minutes.

Makes about 60 cookies.

Chocolate Chip Cookies

1 cup butter
2 cups sugar
2 eggs
1 teaspoon vanilla
2¼ cups soy flour
6 ounces semi-sweet chocolate drops
1 to 2 tablespoons water (if necessary)

Blend in the order given. Drop heaping teaspoonsful of batter onto a greased cookie sheet about 2 inches apart. Bake in a 375° F. oven for 10 to 12 minutes. Remove immediately with a spatula and put on wax paper to cool.

Makes about 40 cookies.

Date Bars

2 eggs, beaten
1 cup sugar
½ teaspoon salt
1 teaspoon vanilla
4 tablespoons water
1 cup soy flour
1 cup pecans or walnuts, chopped fine
1 cup chopped dates
Confectioners' sugar

Beat eggs. Add sugar, salt, vanilla, water, and flour. Mix well and fold in nuts and dates. Spoon onto greased 8-by-16-inch pan and bake at 375° F. for about 30 minutes. Let cool and cut into bars before removing from pan.

If you like, roll each bar in confectioners' sugar when cool.

Makes 32 2-inch squares.

Biscochitos (All-Soy)

1¼ cups soy flour
4 teaspoons cinnamon
⅔ cup shortening
4 egg yolks
⅔ cup sugar
2 tablespoons water
Confectioners' sugar (optional)

Sift cinnamon and flour together. Beat well egg yolks and shortening until fluffy. Add sugar and mix until creamy.

Now add flour mixture and mix thoroughly. Shape into small balls the size of a marble and flatten with palms of hands. Place on a buttered cookie sheet about 1 inch apart. Bake in a moderate (350° F.) oven until edges brown and cookies become easily detached from cookie sheet.

Makes 25 cookies.

If you like, sprinkle cookies with powdered sugar while they are still hot.

Almond Cookies

1½ cups soy flour
1½ cups all-purpose flour
1 teaspoon baking powder
¼ teaspoon salt
1 cup shortening
1½ cups sugar
1 egg, beaten
½ teaspoon vanilla extract
1 teaspoon almond extract
Blanched almonds

Sift together flours, baking powder, and salt. Cream shortening and sugar together. Add beaten egg and vanilla and almond extracts to shortening. Mix together well. Add dry ingredients to form a dough. Knead dough until firm. Roll into small balls (about 1 tablespoon) and flatten on greased cookie sheet. Decorate each cookie with 1 blanched almond.

Bake in a moderate oven (350° F.) for 20 minutes, or until brown.

Makes 60 cookies.

Old-fashioned Oatmeal Cookies

1 cup sugar
½ cup butter
2 eggs
1½ cups milk
2 cups soy flour
1 teaspoon each cinnamon, nutmeg, allspice
1 cup oatmeal
1 cup chopped pecans or walnuts
1 cup raisins
½ teaspoon salt

Blend sugar, butter, and eggs. Add milk, flour, and spices, beating well. Add oatmeal, nuts, raisins, and salt. Drop by teaspoonsful onto a greased cookie sheet about 1½ inches apart. Bake in a 325° to 350° F. oven for about 30 minutes. They should be lightly browned.
Makes 30 cookies.

Soy Pastry

1½ cups all-purpose flour, sifted
½ cup soy flour, sifted
1 teaspoon salt
½ to ¾ cup shortening, more if a more short crust is desired
⅓ to ½ cup cold water

Sift together the flours and salt. Cut in shortening until crumbs are the size of a pea. Add cold water, a few drops at a time, mixing in lightly with a fork. Add only enough water to make a ball that sticks together when pressed gently with as little handling as possible. Chill. Roll to ⅛ inch thickness on a lightly floured surface. Bake in a hot oven (400° F.) for 12 to 15 minutes, or until golden brown in color. Cool, and use with desired pie filling.

You may never have thought it, but I guarantee this pie is going to be a hot rival to your favorite pumpkin pie.

Soybean Pie

1 cup cooked soybeans, drained
¾ cup milk
½ cup honey
¼ teaspoon salt
¼ teaspoon ginger
¼ teaspoon cinnamon
⅛ teaspoon allspice
1 teaspoon grated lemon rind
1 tablepsoon melted butter
4 tablespoons flour
1 9-inch prebaked pie shell or graham cracker crust
Whipped cream (optional)
Candied fruit rinds (optional)

Purée beans in milk in blender. Add other ingredients and mix thoroughly. Heat slowly, stirring constantly, until mixture thickens. Pour into any 9-inch prebaked pie crust or graham cracker crust. Chill thoroughly. May be topped with whipped cream or garnished with finely chopped candied fruit rinds.

Soybean Cream Pie

2 cups soybean purée*
⅔ cup brown sugar
¼ teaspoon salt
1 teaspoon cinnamon
½ teaspoon ginger
½ teaspoon nutmeg
1 cup light cream
2 eggs, beaten
1 tablespoon cognac (or to taste)
9-inch unbaked pie shell

Preheat oven to 350° F.

Combine soybean purée, sugar, salt, cinnamon, ginger, and nutmeg. Gradually beat in cream until smooth. Mix the eggs and cognac together, add to soybean mixture, and mix thoroughly. Turn into pie shell and bake in a preheated oven for 40 minutes, or until center is set.

* Prepare the purée in a food grinder or colander OR use—
Blender method: Purée 2 cups packed beans and light cream in a blender. Add remaining ingredients and continue as above.

It's difficult to believe that anything so delicious could be so nutritious—and vice versa!

Grand Marnier Cream Pie

2 cups soybean purée*
⅔ cup sugar
¼ teaspoon salt
1 cup light cream
2 eggs, beaten
1 tablespoon grated orange rind
⅓ cup Grand Marnier liqueur
   9-inch unbaked pie shell

Preheat oven to 350° F.

Combine soybean purée, sugar, salt, and cream in a bowl. Mix until blended. Add beaten eggs, grated orange rind, and Grand Marnier. Mix thoroughly. Turn into pie shell and bake in a preheated oven for 40 minutes, or until center is set.

Variation: To make an ice-box pie, prepare as above and heat mixture in a double boiler (stirring constantly) until thick—whirls will form. Turn into *baked* pie shell or graham cracker pie shell and chill well.

* Purée in a food grinder or colander OR use—
Blender method: Put 2 cups packed soybeans and all other ingredients into blender. Blend thoroughly and continue as above.

Soybean Custard

    2 eggs
    ½ cup brown sugar, packed
    ¼ teaspoon salt
    ¼ teaspoon nutmeg
    ¼ teaspoon powdered ginger
    1 cup heavy cream
    1 cup cooked soybeans, packed
 1½ tablespoons cognac
 2½ tablespoons grated orange rind
    Ginger-flavored whipped cream to top (optional)

Preheat oven to 325° F.

Put eggs, sugar, salt, nutmeg, ginger, and ½ of cream into a blender and blend well. Add other ingredients and blend thoroughly until creamy. Pour into 6 buttered custard cups. Set in a shallow pan of hot water. Bake in a preheated oven for 30 minutes, or until done. (A knife inserted in the center of custard should come out clean.) Serve warm or chilled. Top with ginger-flavored whipped cream if you like.

Soybean Custard Pie

1½ cups soybean purée*
 3 egg yolks, beaten
 1 cup brown sugar, packed
 ¼ teaspoon salt
 ½ teaspoon powdered ginger
 ½ teaspoon cinnamon
1½ cups sour cream
 2 tablespoons grated orange rind
 3 egg whites, stiffly beaten
 2 9-inch pie shells, baked 10 minutes and cooled
   Whipped cream to top (optional)

* Purée beans in a food grinder or colander OR use—
Blender method: Blend 1½ cups firmly packed soybeans, egg yolks, and sour cream. Add remaining ingredients and continue as above.

Preheat oven to 350° F.
Mix soybean purée, egg yolks, sugar, salt, ginger, and cinnamon. Gradually blend in sour cream. Fold in orange rind and beaten egg whites. Turn into pie shells and bake in a preheated oven for 25 minutes, or until center is set. Serve warm, or cold with whipped cream.

Mexican Pudding

4 cups cooked, firmly packed soybeans, drained
1 cup dark rum (or bourbon)
1 cup mixed candied fruit
1 cup sugar
1 cup water
⅓ cup corn syrup
  Nutmeg (freshly ground if possible)
  Whipped cream

Purée beans in a food grinder, force through a colander, or purée in a blender.*

Combine ½ cup rum and the candied fruit and let stand for 1 or 2 hours.

Combine the sugar, water, and corn syrup, and simmer for 5 minutes. Add this syrup and the candied fruit to the puréed beans. Add the remaining rum and transfer to a glass serving dish. Let stand in the refrigerator for as long as possible, preferably for 2 days before serving. Sprinkle with nutmeg and top with whipped cream.

Serves 6 to 10.

* If using a blender, add the sugar, water, and corn syrup mixture (after cooking) to the beans to facilitate blending. Then add the candied fruit, remaining rum, etc.

Yeast Rolls

2 .6-ounce yeast cakes
1 cup lukewarm water
1 teaspoon salt
1 tablespoon sugar
1 tablespoon melted shortening or vegetable oil
1 egg, beaten
½ cup soy flour, sifted
2⅔ cups all-purpose flour

Dissolve yeast in lukewarm water and let sit for 10 minutes. Add salt, sugar, shortening, egg, and soy flour. Mix well. Add all-purpose flour and yeast. Mix to form a stiff dough. Knead for 10 minutes, adding only enough flour to make handling easy. Let dough rise in a warm place (80° F.) out of drafts until double in bulk. Form into small rolls and place in an oiled muffin pan. Bake at 375° F. for about 15 minutes. Serve hot or cold.

Makes 10 to 12.

Ginger Cookies

    ¾ cup shortening
    1 cup brown sugar, packed
    1 egg
    ¼ cup molasses
    3 tablespoons milk
 2¼ cups soy flour
    2 teaspoons baking powder
    1 teaspoon cinnamon
    1 teaspoon ginger
    ½ teaspoon cloves
    ¼ teaspoon salt
      Granulated sugar to top (optional)

Mix together shortening, brown sugar, egg, molasses, and milk. Then blend in remaining ingredients, mixing together well.

Drop batter in rounded teaspoonsful onto a lightly greased baking sheet. Bake in a 350° oven for 12 to 15 minutes, or until just set. Remove immediately from baking sheet. Sprinkle each cookie (while still hot) with granulated sugar if you so desire.

Makes about 4 dozen.

Coconut Soy Cake

    1 cup all-purpose flour
    ½ cup soy flour
    2 teaspoons baking powder
    ½ teaspoon salt
    1 cup sugar
    1 cup sour cream (or yogurt)
    2 eggs, beaten
    ½ cup vegetable oil

Topping:
½ cup shredded coconut
½ cup chopped nuts
 1 teaspoon cinnamon
¼ cup sugar

Mix topping ingredients together well.
Preheat oven to 350° F.
Sift together flours, baking powder, and salt. Mix other ingredients together and gradually beat in flour mixture. Mix well and pour into a greased cake pan. Sprinkle with topping. Bake in a preheated oven for 35 to 45 minutes.

One of these muffins and a glass of milk would make an extraordinary energy-giving, body-building snack for growing youngsters. And it's great for the lunch box.

Apple and Carrot All-Soy Muffins

2½ cups soy flour
 3 teaspoons baking powder
½ teaspoon salt
 1 teaspoon cinnamon
½ teaspoon allspice
½ teaspoon nutmeg
 1 cup vegetable oil
 1 cup honey
 4 eggs
 1 teaspoon vanilla
 1 cup grated apple
 1 cup grated carrot

Preheat oven to 375° F.
Sift flour, baking powder, salt, cinnamon, allspice, and nutmeg together.

In another bowl combine oil, honey, eggs, and vanilla, beating well. Gradually add dry ingredients and blend until smooth. Fold in grated apples and carrots. Mix well. Spoon into greased muffin pans and bake in a preheated oven for 25 to 35 minutes.

Makes about 2 dozen medium-size muffins.

Apple Schmarren

1 cup soy flour, sifted
⅛ teaspoon salt (or to taste)
2 eggs
1 cup milk
1½ cups coarsely chopped apples
3 tablespoons butter
¼ cup sugar
1 tablespoon cinnamon

Preheat oven to 350° F.

Sift flour and salt together in a bowl. Beat eggs and milk together and add to flour. Beat until smooth, then stir in the apple pieces.

Melt butter in a 9-inch skillet or baking pan and pour the mixture into it.

Bake in a preheated oven for 15 minutes, or until set. Sprinkle with sugar and cinnamon. Tear into small pieces with two forks.

Serves 4.

Custards are always a perfect dessert. This one is easy to make, protein-rich, and delightfully different.

Egg Custard with Soy Granules

¼ cup sugar
½ teaspoon cinnamon
2½ cups milk
2 eggs
1 teaspoon grated lemon rind
½ cup soy granules

Mix sugar and cinnamon. Add milk, eggs, and grated lemon; and beat well until thoroughly blended. Add granules and mix well.

Cook over medium heat, stirring constantly, until mixture thickens. Remove from heat and chill.

Serves 4.

9

❧ ❀ ❧

Soy Milk and Soy Yogurt

Perhaps you've never thought of utilizing soy milk—
it's a creamy white milk containing practically all the nutrients of the soybean. Although it is not *quite* the equal of cow's
milk in total food value, it's nevertheless richer than cow's
milk in iron and phosphorus. It may be used in any recipe
calling for dairy milk.

As a beverage, it is a delightful taste treat. I first dis-
covered soy milk as I was walking in New York's Chinatown.
Seeing the steaming white liquid being served to a group of
Chinese children (who were obviously enjoying it), I be-
came quite curious. Must be something good. But I had no
idea what it was—and there aren't any coconut palms in
that part of town! So I tried some, and found it delicious
from the first taste.

Here are three recipes—all excellent.

THREE METHODS FOR MAKING SOY MILK

Preparation: Wash and pick over 1 pound dried soybeans and soak overnight or longer. Some methods suggest

soaking for at least 24 hours. And remember, 1 pound of dried soybeans makes 3 quarts of soy milk. Compare this with the price of cow's milk!

Grinder Method

Drain the soaked beans and run them through a food grinder, using a fine blade. Put the ground beans in a cheesecloth bag, and tie securely. Submerge bag in 3 quarts warm water and work thoroughly with the hands for 5 to 10 minutes. Wring the bag of ground beans until dry. Boil the milk on a low flame for 30 minutes, stirring frequently to prevent scorching. Add karo syrup, honey, dextrose, or sugar to taste. Add a bit of salt if you like. Cool quickly and refrigerate in tightly covered glass bottles or jars. Use within 2 or 3 days.

Blender Method

Drain the soaked beans. Using the highest speed on your blender, "liquefy" the beans in warm water. It is important to keep account of how much water is used in this process as the total amount of water used for this should not exceed 3 quarts. (I usually liquefy about a cup of beans in 1 cup water. This way all the beans can be liquefied in 6 "batches" using 6 cups, or 1½ quarts water.)

Line a colander with a double layer of fine cheesecloth and strain liquid into a pan. Wring mash in cheesecloth until dry. Add 1½ quarts hot water to liquid in pan and boil over low flame for 30 minutes, stirring frequently to avoid scorching. Add karo syrup, honey, dextrose, or sugar to taste. Add a bit of salt if you like. Cool quickly and refrigerate in tightly covered glass bottles or jars. Use within 2 or 3 days.

Quick Method

Drain soaked beans and run them through a food grinder, using a fine blade. In a saucepan, add 3 quarts boiling water to the ground beans. Bring mixture to a boil and simmer for 15 minutes. Line a colander with a double layer of fine cheesecloth and strain liquid into a pan or bowl. Wring mash in cheesecloth until dry. Add karo syrup, honey, dextrose, or sugar to taste. Add a bit of salt if you like. Cool quickly and refrigerate in tightly covered glass bottles or jars. Use within 2 or 3 days.

If you wish to make less than 3 quarts of milk, use the following proportions:

3⅓ cups soaked beans (unground) to 1½ quarts water
OR 1¾ cups soaked beans (unground) to 3 cups water.

The ground bean pulp (or mash) has too much nutritive value to be thrown away. Remember, you can combine it with other foods—particularly with foods or dishes having a pronounced flavor. Use it in soups, stews, meat loaves, patties, or stuffings. But do use it within 2 or 3 days. It can also be frozen for later use.

SOY YOGURT

Soy yogurt—not surprisingly—is made from soy milk. It can be served plain or sweetened with honey, syrup, or marmalades. Or try it served over fresh fruit for a healthful dessert or snack.

If you have a yogurt maker, the preparation is identical to that of dairy yogurt. Simply substitute soy milk for cow's milk and proceed as usual. I recommend yogurt makers for those who eat yogurt regularly. They are quite fool-proof and pay for themselves in a matter of a few weeks.

If you *don't* have a yogurt maker, prepare as follows:

Heat 1 quart soy milk to the boiling point. Remove from heat and cool for 30 minutes. Add 2 or 3 tablespoons dairy yogurt or 1 package yogurt culture. Mix well, pour into sterilized jars and seal. Keep in a warm place (or place a jar over the pilot light on the stove—this works just as well) for 2 or 3 hours, or until mixture reaches desired consistency. Save 2 or 3 tablespoons of yogurt to start your next batch.

List of Products and Seasonings Not Generally Used in Western Cooking

The following ingredients are called for in the Japanese and Chinese recipes in the chapters on tofu and bean sprouts:

Soy Sauce is the most essential ingredient in Oriental cuisine. There is no substitute for its flavor. There are several brands of domestic soy sauce available that are good. However, I strongly recommend the Japanese soy sauce.

Monosodium Glutamate (MSG) can be found in most supermarkets under such trade names as "Accent" or "Zest." A small amount enhances the natural flavors of meat and vegetables. Most of the Japanese and Chinese recipes included here call for it. Interestingly enough, the first MSG was extracted from a soybean preparation. Nowadays, most MSG in the United States is a by-product of beet-sugar refining.

Fresh Ginger Root can be found in most Oriental markets. If it is impossible to find, use powdered ginger—but only half of what the recipe calls for in fresh ginger. If you are not familiar with the taste of ginger, use some caution until you have developed a taste for it.

Sesame Oil is amber in color and has a most distinct flavor and bouquet. It is used (in small amounts) in many Oriental dishes. It can be found in most Oriental markets or health food stores.

Sherry is not foreign to most cooks, of course. A good quality dry sherry (cooking sherry will not give the proper flavor) makes an acceptable substitute for yellow rice wine. Many Chinese recipes call for it.

Mirin is a sweet rice wine essential to good Japanese cuisine. It can be found in Oriental markets or some health food stores.

Miso is a fermented paste made of cooked soybeans, yeast, salt, and sometimes, rice. It is very important in Japanese cuisine. It is sold in plastic pouches or cans. If refrigerated, it will keep for a year or more. Most health food markets and Oriental markets keep it in stock.

Aka-miso—red bean paste—is available in Oriental markets.

Hanagatsuo is the shavings of dried bonito fish. It is a basic ingredient for dashi—the Japanese soup stock. Oriental markets and health food stores stock it in cellophane packets.

Kombu is dried kelp. It is one of the two basic ingredients in Japanese soup stock, or dashi. Sold in health food stores and Oriental markets.

Dashi. Either follow the simple recipe on page 106 or buy one of the several brands of instant dashi on the market. They are quite good and come in small packets that usually make one cup of dashi each.

Suppliers of Foreign Food Products

If you cannot always obtain some of the ingredients called for in the preceeding recipes, you might try writing to one of the suppliers listed below who is in your region.

JAPANESE

Enbun Company, 248 East 1st Street, Los Angeles, California 90012.

Modern Food Market, 140 South San Pedro Street, Los Angeles, California 90012.

Pacific Mercantile Company, 1946 Larimer Street, Denver, Colorado 80202.

House of Hanna, 1468 T Street, N.W., Washington, D.C. 20009.

Tropi Pak Food Products, 3664 Northwest 48th Street, Miami, Florida 33142.

Franklin Food Store, 1309 East 53rd Street, Chicago, Illinois 60650.

Imported Foods, 1038 McCormick, Wichita, Kansas 67213.

Oriental Trading Company, 2636 Edenborn Avenue, Metairie, Louisiana 70002.

Yoshinoya, 36 Prospect Street, Cambridge, Massachusetts 02139.

Kado's Oriental Imports, 251 Merrill, Birmingham, Michigan 48011.

Maruyama's, 100 North 18th Street, St. Louis, Missouri 63103.

Oriental Trading Company, 1115 Farnam Street, Omaha, Nebraska 68102.

Japanese Foodland, 2620 Broadway, New York, New York 10025.

Japanese Mart, 239 West 105th Street, New York, New York 10025.

Katagiri Company, 224 East 59th Street, New York, New York 10022.

Nippon Do, 82-69 Parsons Boulevard, Jamaica, New York 11432.

Oriental Food Shop, 1302 Amsterdam Avenue, New York, New York 10027.

Tanaka and Company, 326 Amsterdam Avenue, New York, New York 10023.

Soya Food Products, 2356 Wyoming Avenue, Cincinnati, Ohio 45214.

Omura Japanese Food and Gift Shop, 3811 Payne Avenue, Cleveland, Ohio 44114.

Anzen Importers, 736 Northeast Union Avenue, Portland, Oregon 97232.

Sage Farm Market, 52 West 1st Street, Salt Lake City, Utah 84101.

Uwajimaya, Inc., 422 South Main Street, Seattle, Washington 98104.

CHINESE

Kwong On Lung Company, 686 North Spring Street, Los Angeles, California 90012.

Wing Chong Lung Company, 922 South San Pedro Street, Los Angeles, California 90015.

Manley Produce, 1101 Grant Avenue, San Francisco, California 94133.

Shing Chong and Company, 800 Grant Avenue, San Francisco, California 94108.

Kam Shing Company, 2246 South Wentworth Avenue, Chicago, Illinois 60616.

Shiroma, 1058 West Argyle Street, Chicago, Illinois 60640.

Wing Wing Imported Groceries, 79 Harrison Avenue, Boston, Massachusetts 02111.

Legal Sea Foods Market, 237 Hampshire Street, Cambridge, Massachusetts 02139.

Eastern Trading Company, 2801 Broadway, New York, New York 10025.

Wing Fat Company, 35 Mott Street, New York, New York 10013.

Wo Fat Company, 16 Bowery, New York, New York 10013.

Yuet Hing Market, Inc., 23 Pell Street, New York, New York 10013.

Oriental Import-Export Company, 2009 Polk Street, Houston, Texas 77003.

MEXICAN AND SOUTH AMERICAN

Del Rey Spanish Foods, Stall A-7, Central Market, 317 South Broadway, Los Angeles, California 90013.

Jurgenson's, 1071 Glendon Avenue, Los Angeles, California 90024.

Casa Lucas Market, 2934 24th Street, San Francisco, California 94110.

Mi Rancho Market, 3365 20th Street, San Francisco, California 94110.

American Tea, Coffee and Spice Company, 1511 Champa Street, Denver, Colorado 80202.

Pena's Spanish Store, 1636 17th Street, N.W., Washington, D.C. 20009.

The Delicatessen, Burdine's Dadeland Shopping Center, Miami, Florida 33156.

Epicure Markets, 1656 Alton Road, Miami Beach, Florida 33139.

La Preferida, Inc., 177-181 West South Water Market, Chicago, Illinois 60608.

Marshall Field and Company, 111 North State Street, Chicago, Illinois 60602.

El-Nopal Food Market, 544 North Highland Avenue, Indianapolis, Indiana 46202.

Swiss Colony, Lindale Plaza, Cedar Rapids, Iowa 52402.

Central Grocery Company, 923 Decatur Street, New Orleans, Louisiana 70116.

Progress Grocery Company, 915 Decatur Street, New Orleans, Louisiana 70116.

Cardullo's Gourmet Shop, 6 Brattle Street, Cambridge, Massachusetts, 02138.

La Paloma-Tenorio and Company, 2620 Bagley Avenue, Detroit, Michigan 48216.

Heidi's Around the World Food Shop, 1149 South Brentwood Boulevard, St. Louis, Missouri 63117.

Casa Moneo Spanish Imports, 210 West 14th Street, New York, New York 10011.

Spanish and American Food Market, 7001 Wade Park Avenue, Cleveland, Ohio 44103.

Heintzelman's, 1128 Northway Mall, Pittsburgh, Pennsylvania 15237.

Morris Zager, 230 Fourth Avenue North, Nashville, Tennessee 37207.

Antone's Import Company, Box 3352, Houston, Texas 77001.

Jamail's, 3114 Kirby Drive, Houston, Texas 77006.

Pier L Imports, 5403 South Rice Avenue, Houston, Texas 77036.

Index